Ian Hibell, possibly Britain's most outstanding touring cyclist, has been honoured by the Cyclists Touring Club for his important contributions to the sport. He gained the taste for adventure during his RAF service in the 1950s, and in 1963 he left Brixham in Devon determined to see more of the world. Since then he has ridden, pushed or carried a bike more than a quarter of a million miles in some of the most inaccessible of places, narrowly missing death on more than one occasion. In between trips he is based in Devon.

Clinton Trowbridge, whose family came from Wiltshire, was a Professor of English at Dowling College in New York. He has written other travel books, including *The Man Who Walked Around the World* (with David Kunst) and *The Crow Island Journal*.

Into The Remote Places

IAN HIBELL AND CLINTON TROWBRIDGE

SPHERE BOOKS LIMITED
London and Sydney

First published in Great Britain by
Robson Books Ltd 1984
Copyright © 1984 Ian Hibell and Clinton Trowbridge
Published by Sphere Books Ltd 1985
30-32 Gray's Inn Road, London WC1X 8JL

The names of some of the characters mentioned in this book, and of some of the English places, have been changed to help preserve privacy.

For Laura

TRADE
MARK

This book is sold subject to the condition that it shall not, by way of trade or otherwise, be lent, re-sold, hired out or otherwise circulated without the publisher's prior consent in any form of binding or cover other than that in which it is published and without a similar condition including this condition being imposed on the subsequent purchaser.

Printed and bound in Great Britain by
Cox & Wyman Ltd, Reading

CONTENTS

1. THE DARIEN GAP   1
2. THE NOR/AFRICA TOUR   39
3. THE PERUVIAN GAP   119

I would like to say thank you to the multi-racial people worldwide for their universal help and friendship. The 'Cyclists' Touring Club' for much encouragement. The Editors of 'Cycling', Ken Evans and Martin Ayres for first giving my experiences an airing. My special thanks to my sponsors who eased the financial outlay considerably and supplied such durable equipment.

Arthur Needham	ARGOS CYCLES, BRISTOL Two excellent indestructible 'special' touring frames.
Middlemores (Coventry) Ltd	SHIMANO Help with considerable equipment and back up on the tour.
Ian Powys	MICHELIN TYRE COMPANY Using their hard wearing tyres I have yet to have a serious blow out.
Sam Braxton	BRAXTON BIKE SHOP, MISSOULA, MONTANA My first good fairy who generously supplied Campagnola spares for the earlier tours and built the wheels used in the Peruvian Gap. Not a single spoke breakage.
Neville Chadwick	CARRADICE OF NELSON, LANCS Kindly provided 'Overlander' bags to my own dimensions and design. An excellent product.
The late Mr Reynolds	MESSRS. R.E.W. REYNOLDS, NORTHAMPTON Over the years supplied superb shoes.
Tent Makers	SIERRA DESIGNS, OAKLAND, CALIFORNIA Over 20 years I have tested their tents under all conditions and have yet to be let down.

I must not forget my friends Stan Lofthouse and John West who were an untiring back up team long before I received any other support.

Lastly thanks to my son Jamie; our first tour together, all of half a mile, was the most exciting nerve racking adventure of all.

Part 1
The Darien Gap

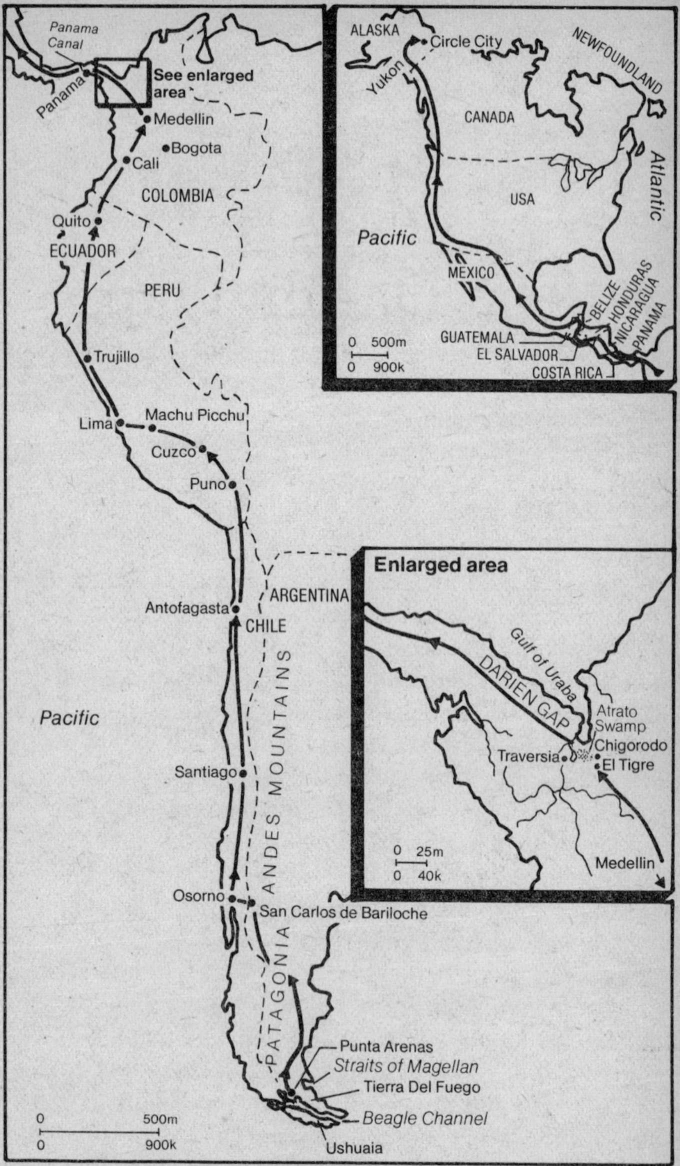

Panama Canal
Panama
See enlarged area
Medellin
Bogota
Cali
COLOMBIA
Quito
ECUADOR
PERU
Trujillo
Lima
Machu Picchu
Cuzco
Puno
ARGENTINA
Antofagasta
CHILE
Pacific
ANDES MOUNTAINS
Santiago
Osorno
San Carlos de Bariloche
PATAGONIA
Punta Arenas
Straits of Magellan
Tierra Del Fuego
Beagle Channel
Ushuaia
0 500m
0 900k
ALASKA
Circle City
Yukon
NEWFOUNDLAND
CANADA
Atlantic
USA
Pacific
MEXICO
BELIZE
HONDURAS
NICARAGUA
PANAMA
GUATEMALA
EL SALVADOR
COSTA RICA
0 500m
0 900k
Enlarged area
Gulf of Uraba
DARIEN GAP
Atrato Swamp
Chigorodo
Traversia
El Tigre
Medellin
0 25m
0 40k

Chapter One

'David!' I called out, and tried my best to go faster, only to fall forward, sinking to my waist. I was certain he'd been bitten by a snake. He squatted there on his haunches, his machete stuck into the bog at his feet, his face drained of all colour. Then he raised his head and stared at us, his eyes blank. Should you give the injection first, or slash the bite and apply the tourniquet? And who had the kit? Steve was examining him.

'Nothing wrong with the bugger,' he said, standing. 'He's all done in, that's all.'

I was too exhausted to show my relief, but even as the image of disaster dissolved it was replaced by dread. If David couldn't keep it up, what were we going to do? He'd cut only about a hundred metres. At that rate we wouldn't make five hundred today, a fourth of what we counted on. For the first time since we'd got ourselves into this mess, I realized with considerable clarity that we might indeed die in here, as so many had predicted. 'We'll have to bring the time down,' I said. 'An hour's too long.'

'Bring it *down?*' sneered Steve. 'When did you last cut at all?'

'Half-hour shifts. Camp man carries up the cycles,' I continued, as if I hadn't heard him.

'You miserable little mucker! You bloody Pom! Who are you to be giving orders?'

I felt myself tense up, the way I had so many times before with Steve, but nothing came out. He picked up the machete and strode off to where the raw edge of the cut stood out against the soft green of the surrounding bush. David had shut his eyes and I knew that he was concentrating on his own condition now – as if the bell had just rung and he had only those few minutes to get himself back together before going out into the ring again for another round. I'd never seen him fight, but he'd described this to me often enough. That one minute was your life. You could pump it into you or you could let it all dribble away. It was entirely up to you.

I could follow Steve. I could grab his machete when he brought it back for a swing, threaten him with it. But then what? He would just rip it out of my hands and laugh at me. It would be like that time in the desert when I told him we could jettison our extra water, that the station was less than an hour away, and Steve had refused. 'Dump it out!' I'd said. So he'd dumped it on my head. And I didn't do a damn thing. What could I have done? Steve was a brute! Six feet tall, hands the size of hams. He could have pushed me right down into the sand with one arm if he'd felt like it. I'd just stood there, dripping, and he'd ridden off, and David had followed him; and Steve's laugh had rung in my ears for days afterward.

But I got even with him that time. For the next two days I set such a pace that Steve was literally crying for me to slow down. All the way to Medellín, in fact, I pushed them. David kept up, but Steve couldn't. For days at a time we hardly saw him. And when we got there, it was I who did all the planning. I was the map expert. I was the one they talked to at the consulate. No, as long as I had a bike under me I was all right. It was the other times that gave me trouble, and we'd been slogging through this swamp now for twenty days.

The worst thing was that Steve was right. A few minutes of cutting and I'd have to rest. For the past five days, I'd been the camp man: cook the rice, set up the hammocks, carry the gear up to the head of the cut; and they'd done all the cutting between them, plus carrying their own bikes and rucksacks. But how I hated him for saying it. How happy it would have made me to see him fall, cry out with exhaustion, pain: the stupid, brutish sheep farmer; all muscle, all appetite; the clumsiest, most careless rider I'd ever known. How many times had I carried his gear for him? How often had I rebuilt his damned wheel because he refused to keep his eyes on the road and was always crashing into pot-holes and running over rocks? If only he'd said: 'Ian, now look. You're not as strong as we are. You're fifteen years older, for one thing. You've got a fine pair of legs, but there's not such a lot of you from the waist up . . . ' but he hadn't said that, had he?

I passed by David and over to where Steve was whacking away at the bush. 'I say,' I said, and he turned a scornful, sweat-streaked face toward me. 'I'll cut at the noon break. I'll cut first thing in the morning. We've got to use all the daylight.'

'Blow off!' said Steve, and turned his back.

That was it. The expedition was leaderless now. It was every man for himself.

The Atrato Swamp in Colombia has never been crossed by foot. Perhaps that is because no one has even been foolish enough to attempt it. It stretches for a hundred kilometres inland from the Gulf of Uraba on the Caribbean, and is approximately the same distance wide. A network of rivers and streams and bogs and tall grasses, it is rumoured to be without bottom. At one time the National Geographic Society supported an expedition to discover whether it was feasible to get through the area. It had been reported they'd dropped a cement block with cable attached into a likely-looking spot and watched it go out of sight. At last record, it had descended three thousand feet and was still sinking. Plans for building a highway through this morass go from dumping millions of tons of a specially porous gravel into the proposed roadbed to floating a causeway across on pontoons. But the project has always seemed too risky, not to say expensive, and this major obstacle to the completion of the Pan American Highway has yet to be bridged.

When we got to El Tigre, the jumping-off spot for the swamp, we discovered that an eight-kilometre road existed. Beyond that, however, the track soon became a slash pile of trees. We had a map, of sorts, prepared by a mining company that had actually pushed in a distance of forty kilometres. Every once in a while, there was a rotted helicopter platform that provided a luxury campsite. Bent double under our 85-pound packs – we had to return for our cycles – we attempted to manoeuvre along this roadbed of slippery tree trunks without either sliding off into the surrounding ooze or disturbing the rest of one of the several varieties of poisonous snakes that inhabit this region. It was not an easy task, but after ten days we arrived at the 36-kilometre post. This was the end of the slash cut. There was an island here, a small community of Indians. To go beyond this point meant cutting our own track – through clumps of dead palms, twelve-foot high grasses and thickets of hardwoods that would dull our machetes in a dozen blows. Was this as far as we could get, then? It seemed so. And we were out of food.

What we finally decided to do was to send Steve back in an outboard with one of the Indians for more supplies. David and myself would take turns cutting the track. When Steve returned the next day, we would decide whether or not to go on.

That first day we made only 400 metres. The next day we rose before dawn, vowing to redouble our efforts. David chopped through the first clump of hardwoods and crossed over the next bog by throwing the brush out in front of him. There was a kind of matted weed here that would support one's weight. During my turn, all I had to cut was grass. By noon we had gone almost one kilometre. There were stretches of boggy flats where there was virtually nothing to cut at all. Late that afternoon, I went back to ferry up the rest of the gear feeling almost light-hearted, so pleased was I with the day's work, when

I noticed that the track, relatively so firm before, was now two inches deep in water. By the time I began my return it was getting dark.

Weighed down with the rucksack, I sometimes plunged chest-deep into the ooze. After a while it was all I could do to crawl out. The hammocks, the other rucksack and our bicycles were with David at the cut. In my pack were the cooking utensils, the stove, and our clothes. I had no food, no protection for the night. As darkness fell I called out for David. I called and called, but there was no response. It rained for a while, a downpour that came in sheet after sheet and was surprisingly cold; and then the jungle began to steam once more and the mosquitoes descended. When I say 'descended', the image of a massive form settling itself down on top of me is exactly the one I wish to convey. It was as if a blanket covered me, but a blanket of stinging nettles, of sea urchins, of porcupines. And it was not the pain only, but the incessant buzzing, enough to drive a monk mad. The impulse to run was as overwhelming as it was, practically speaking, impossible. That night I became a friend of water, a companion to mud. I burrowed myself into the swamp and lay there, alligator-like, breathing through a matting of brush that discouraged all but the hardiest of mosquitoes from flying down my windpipe.

When morning finally came and I was able to plunge on along the track, I was almost dead. How good it was to be reunited. 'Thought you'd never see me again, did you?' I managed to get out.

'You pommy bastard. How d'ya expect me to cook without the pots?' But David's smile belied his words. We set up then and there and boiled the last of the rice. Steve returned late that afternoon.

'Why didn't ya carry this up for me, eh?' he growled, and threw his bike down. But we were too glad to see him to react. The outboard had broken down, he told us. But all we could think of was what he'd brought for our dinner: canned beef and peaches! The first meal we'd had of anything but rice for a week. We gorged. Steve was our saviour. We were comrades, comrades in arms.

The next day, the jungle closed in on us again and even with Steve's help, we cut only 700 metres. That night we camped at the 40-kilometre post completely unsure about what to do. The next part was the worst of all. Not only would we have to cut our own track, but now we would have to do so on a strict compass bearing. There were twenty kilometres between us and the tiny village of Traversia on an island in the Atrato River. If we failed to come out on to the bank exactly opposite that only post of civilization in the area, we would not know whether to look for it up river or down. And by then we would not have the strength to walk any further.

This was the point of no return. If we went on now we were committed to going all the way. For there would not be enough food to get us back.

Wordlessly we set up camp. We knew nothing about what lay ahead. It might be so marshy we could not walk. Or dense jungle. We had to average two kilometres a day or we would run out of food. Would there be trees to hang our hammocks from? Would we even find a place to set up our primus stove? The sensible thing, of course, was to admit defeat, and begin the long trek back to El Tigre in the morning. But at first light we pushed on. None of us, I think, could bear the thought that our year-and-a-half struggle up through South America had been a waste of time.

Chapter Two

'If you must die, please arrange to do so in Panama.' Those were the friendly parting words of the honorary British consul in Medellín. Of all our advisers only Michael Hill, the local entomologist and expert on the Atrato, gave us any chance. He even took the trouble to describe what a certain rare orchid looked like in case we chanced to come upon it. Long before, when we first made inquiries, we were informed that the whole Darien Gap – an area 400 kilometres long, stretching from a hundred kilometres inside Colombia to the Panama Canal was impassable. As usual, however, the thing itself proved to be nowhere near as bad as it had been described to us. Hill assured us that if we got to the Atrato River, we would find smugglers' trails. What everyone else agreed on, however, was the impossibility of our getting to the Atrato at all. For one thing, it was late in the season. The rains could begin at any time. One look at the high-water mark on the trees told us what would be our fate if we were caught by them. And what if we came upon stretches of water too wide for us to swim, too deep to wade through? There might be rivers, large streams. The Atrato River itself was half a mile wide. No one had been into the area except in boats. Oh, there was plenty of water all right.

But we made preparations. We brought a truck inner tube, a pump, and 400 metres of nylon cord. With this crude raft, we could haul ourselves across the largest stretches of water. In Medellín, thanks to the kindness of the owner of a garden pond, we practised with the tube and line, while curious townspeople gathered behind the bushes: the crazy Englishman and his two New Zealand companions. The tube would support either one bike or one fully-loaded pack, we discovered. How it would behave in swifter water we could only guess.

We had taken a two-day trip to Bogota to get our

supplies, snake serum, and our all-important jungle hammocks; and we were about ready to go when a truck ran over Steve's foot and broke it. Or so, at first, it seemed. Though X-rays showed it was only badly sprained, he would be in a cast for a week. Then something even worse happened.

As far back as Trujillo, fifteen hundred kilometres away, we had read in the paper that a British Army Range-Rover Team was planning to cross the Darien Gap about the same time we were. They were en route from Alaska to Tierra del Fuego – our own journey only in reverse. The news spurred us on all the faster. Then, as we got closer and found out more about conditions in the Atrato Swamp, we became less apprehensive. Clearly there was no way even a Range-Rover could drive through such a place. They would have to transport their vehicles around, as had the two other expeditions that had passed through the area. As it was our intention to walk every inch of the way we could not actually cycle, we no longer saw ourselves in competition with them. When we had to depend on a boat – or our inner tube – to cross a river, we would make certain that our passage was from shore to opposite shore, not up or down vast stretches of waterway. But then we met Captain Jeremy Sharp.

Sharp was the liaison officer for the British Army expedition, and he calmly told us that it was his assignment to get to the village of Traversia and reconnoitre a possible route from there to El Tigre. So the British Army really intended to push through. The race was on. If Captain Sharp and his crew were successful, they would be the first human beings to walk through the Atrato Swamp. They would have accomplished the impossible, not us. And to get to Traversia, Captain Sharp had the use of a Colombian gunboat and a crew of Colombian soldiers. The day before Steve sprained his foot, Captain Sharp had left for the port of Turbo, on the Caribbean. 'Good luck,' he had shouted. 'And may the best man win.'

But an ugly fate played into our hands. The very evening before our own long-awaited departure, Sharp returned to Medellín. We did not see him. He did not seek us out. What had happened was this: he had gathered his supplies together and left a Colombian officer in charge of transporting them to the gunboat which was moored some distance out in the bay. The man was using a twelve-foot aluminium dinghy, and Sharp was concerned at the time that he was loading it too heavily. Not wanting to interfere, however, he had decided to trust to luck. All went well. And then came the final trip. They had no more than started out into the bay when a wave came aboard; and in a matter of seconds the boat sank. Sharp himself only just managed to swim ashore, having been forced to strip off his clothes in order to avoid being pulled under by the clawing arms of one of his men. Of the Colombian soldiers, only the officer could swim. It was many days before all the bodies were recovered. The last ones to drift ashore were unrecognizable: eyes eaten out by crabs, flesh slashed to the bone by predators, features horribly distorted.

Early the following morning we left Medellín, no longer in competition with Captain Sharp and his crew, but under the pall of his tragedy.

I lunged at the dead palm frond with all my strength and felt the machete turn in my hand. It bounced off the hard stem and sliced into my left shin. There! I thought. Now I've done it, as I fell backward into the muck. For a second or two I lay still, not daring to move; and then the pain cleared my head and I realized I hadn't cut my leg off after all and that I had better do something fast to stop the bleeding.

Dimly, in the background, I could hear Steve's voice. I tore a piece of cloth off my shirt and tied it around the wound as firmly as I could, then lay there watching the blood welling up through the bandage for what seemed ages, until at last it began to cake over. Steve was nearby – I could hear his grunts and the chomping sound his machete made on the entangled growth. By the time I got up the strength to crawl after them, I could hear the sound of the machete only as a dull thudding in the distance. All afternoon I pulled myself along the track, sometimes up to my neck in water, sometimes thrashing alligator-like through the clinging mud. Only the dread of being left alone when darkness came made me able to go on.

Steve and David were hunched over their bowls of rice when I finally caught up with them. Neither one said a word. All night the throbbing pain in my leg kept me awake and all night I reaffirmed my vow that I would keep on going.

Before they left the next morning, David came over to where I was lying in my hammock and offered me a torn-off bit of shirt sleeve. I accepted it but I did not speak. After they had gone, I carefully peeled off the blood-stiffened rag and examined my wound. It was a deep gash, showing the bone. I had torn the cut loose, and the wound was bleeding, but it did not seem to be inflamed. I bound it up again with what David had given me and steeled myself for what was to come. The day before I had nothing to carry but myself. Now there was my hammock, my bicycle, and my rucksack. There was a pot with some rice in it next to where the previous night's meal had been cooked. I gobbled it down with trembling fingers. It was the first 'meal' I'd had since the preceding morning. Stuffing the hammock and the pot into my otherwise empty rucksack, leaning heavily on my bicycle, I prepared to leave. The track before me resembled an overgrown drainage ditch during the worst times of the rainy season. I had cycled countless miles alongside such ditches in Malaysia and Indonesia. Little had I thought then I'd ever be slogging my way up through the middle of one.

All day long I was alone. If I did not make it to the head

of the cut by nightfall, I was sure I would not be missed. Once, however, I caught a glimpse of David. He was crossing a muck hole and I saw him disappear. The top of his head broke the surface and an arm flailed wildly, then vanished. The steaming cauldron surged and the arm rose again, this time successfully. As he slowly, painfully, dragged himself out, he reached back down into the pit for his bicycle and his eyes met mine. They were as cold as any snake's. I had watched him struggle for his life and, even though he had once been my friend, I felt only the most complete detachment.

'I can see you're not cut out for this job,' David had said, and then he had walked away, leaving me there, stuttering. It was 6 a.m., the end of my first night's shift at the New Zealand wool factory, and David was my overseer. All night long, every half hour or so, he would come into the wool room and glare at me. Well, I was working as fast as I could. You couldn't ass around. I was running my bloody legs off. But that wasn't fast enough. I couldn't keep the hoppers full, and that meant that David had difficulty in maintaining the right moisture level of the scoured wool. Maybe he thought that by coming in and looking at me as if I were a bit of turd floating around the rim of the toilet bowl, I would pick up the pace. All I can say is that if Hercules himself had been in my place, he couldn't have done it fast enough to please David Ferris.

Ten days later he spoke to me for the second time. 'Heard you bicycled out from England,' he said.

'Yep,' I replied. End of conversation. And then one night, it must have been a month later, he appeared at the Clive youth hostel where I was warden. There was a cosy fire blazing and a fellow from Belgium was telling us about an adventure he'd had with some head-hunters in Borneo. It was similar to something that had happened to me there and I was listening to him intently. It gave me a surprise when I noticed David standing off to one side.

When the story was finished I expected him to come over and say something. But he didn't. He just stood there, at the edge of the firelight, and an hour or so later he left, as silently and mysteriously as he'd arrived. Every once in a while during the next three or four months he would suddenly turn up like that. And it was always the same. He'd never say a word or actually join the group.

By then we were building a hostel out at Lake Tutire. At the end of one of the wool factory shifts, he overheard me complaining I had no way of getting out there for the weekend. 'I'll give you a ride,' he said. A few days later he moved into the hostel. Seems he'd been looking for a better place to live. He proved to be a good worker and little by little, to my great surprise, we became friends. It wasn't long after that he asked if he could join up on my Cape Horn to Alaska tour.

David had never ridden a bicycle for more than a mile or two at a stretch. But he'd worked on his uncle's sheep farm for most of his life, and he was fit as can be and very determined. His problem, I discovered, was that he had missed being New Zealand's amateur welter-weight boxing champion by just one point. Three drinks in a pub and he tried to take on everyone in the house. He looked like a boxer, too: pushed-up nose, tough-looking mug, his whole body square and solid as a brick; but he was short, almost as short as I was, and he couldn't put two sentences together to save his neck. He needed something he could test himself against, he said. Well, I could understand that.

I found out how determined he was the first time we raced. We'd been in training about a month, and one day I put out a bit more than usual just to see if he had it in him yet. And I was surprised. He was keeping right up with me, and I had him on a low gear, too, to get his legs supple. We were pumping away up a long hill when I noticed that David's face had turned red. Beet-red. His expression hadn't altered the least bit, though. It was the same lock-jawed, granite-mouthed puss he shoved at the boys in the pub. I slowed to a stop and got off the bike. 'Time for a break,' I said, and he grinned lopsidedly. 'Thought I was done for, eh?' He could hardly get the words out. But he'd been right at the popping point. I could see that.

'You should take up racing,' I said. 'You'd have yourself a career.' His grin was more normal now. That's what I wanted in a companion, I thought, as we rode on. What did I care for conversational ability?

As for Steve, I felt sorry for him at first. He'd been thrown off the family farm by his father and told never to come back. He was only twenty-two and when he told the story of what had happened to him, his blue eyes lit up, his expression became very sincere, and you felt certain that he had been wronged. He was alone in the world. That's why he was at the hostel. What he wanted was an adventure – something exciting. He wasn't competitive, like David. If we got going too fast for him, he just lagged behind. But he was as strong as the proverbial ox. He'd pick me up by the waist and hold me in the air, squeezing, till I'd yell 'uncle'. His shoulders were as broad as David's and mine put together.

However, I thought that it was his kind of strength we would need when we got to the Darien Gap. And I turned out to be right about that, at least.

Chapter Three

I lifted my cycle clear of the matted weeds and pushed it out in front of me. Would it support my weight or bring me face down into the water? It held, and I dragged myself forward another foot. Lift. Thrust. Lean. Lurch. My cycle? My crutch. My companion. Helpless would I be without it. Once, I regained consciousness to find myself lying on the frame, head held above the water only by the accident of its having hit the edge of the seat. Had the sudden wrenching of my leg caused me to black out? I don't know, but it was certainly the case that I placed no weight on it at all, now. If I was following in the wake of David and Steve my leg was following in the wake of me. I had not looked at my cut for three days. Continuously immersed in water, it could not heal. At night the bandage would stiffen. It would be hard and crusted in the morning, but after a few minutes in the swamp, tiny trails of blood would trickle out around it. Whether the cut had opened again, or this was simply coagulated blood liquifying and dispersing, I never did discover. However, my leg had not begun to swell. All night it throbbed. But during the day I was mostly oblivious of the pain, my whole attention being focussed on the track.

When I fell, when the cycle disappeared into nothingness and I pulled myself, spluttering, out of the water, I would lie there for a moment. Not too long, though, for starting up again was difficult in direct proportion to the time I allowed myself to rest – as if there were whole freight trains of me to get on the move. What I tried to do was take three steps in a row, count to twenty, take three more steps, count to twenty, and so on. It was imperative that I keep up as fast a pace as I was able. The image of the night I had spent alone on the track, huddled in the mud, was all too vivid in my memory.

Lift. Thrust. Lean. Lurch. Again the grasses held. We had to be near the river. It was our 25th day. For the last twenty-four hours we had had nothing to eat but oatmeal: two handfuls for breakfast, two for dinner. In one more day that would be gone. I noticed a leech hanging from my thigh where the flesh showed through my torn pants. Squeezing its squirming body between my thumb and forefinger, I felt the sharp pain as I pulled it off. Its head was still there, embedded in my flesh. By evening the spot would have swollen and turned red. How many more leeches clung to me? In my hammock, at night, I would go through the ritual of inspection, but for a long time now we had not bothered to check our bodies during the day. Our feet and lower legs were inflamed and scaly-looking, an advanced stage of trench foot; and our bodies itched and festered from the countless bites and scratches. The hammock was our only refuge. We stood waist-deep in water even while preparing our food, one of us holding up the primus while the cook stirred the rice. But now there was no rice, only oatmeal, and we were too exhausted to cook that.

By my calculations we were very near the river, however; within a kilometre, surely. Would we come out at the village, though? I hardly dared think about that.

Two days before I'd cut my leg, a helicopter had flown over us. The first pass he took we had waved our arms and cheered. 'What about it, mates?' I'd said. 'Do we let him take us out?' There was a longish pause.

'Bugger him off,' said Steve.

'David?'

'Guess not.'

How many times since then I'd wished we hadn't been so heroic. But to be lifted out, to be carried like babies back to El Tigre: the laughing-stock, the butt of all jokes; at the time, even to me, that seemed unacceptable.

The pilot made three passes. When he flew over for the second time and we waved him away, he wheeled up and hovered there for a minute, as if waiting for us to change our minds. If he'd let down a rope, if he'd opened the door, even; maybe then it would have been different. But there was something about the too-bright shimmer of the smooth, metallic underbelly that made us refuse his offer. We had started up again and we didn't give him any signal at all when he came past for the third time. He whirred over, not thirty feet above us, rose, banked around, and then, with a little rocking motion, sped off in the direction of El Tigre. It was that good-bye that got to me, that suggestion of good luck. Who was he, who was anyone, to wish us well in a place like that?

And then the emptiness, the silence. No sound except the buzz of insects, the flutterings and cawings of a few birds. Nothing overhead but the glaring sun beating down through the milky haze of a festering sky; nothing in any direction but swamp grass, low stands of hardwoods, palmetto shrubs, and the ever-present water. And for miles and miles there was no other human being, no sign of even the most rudimentary form of human life; only in front of us, somewhere, this Indian village on an island in the Atrato. If the helicopter had returned half an hour later it would have found us begging for deliverance. We did not speak for the remainder of that afternoon. The machete's steady ring was like a metronome. It was the worst point of the whole trip for me, up till then; a sense of desolation more complete than I'd ever experienced before.

Lift. Thrust. Lean. Lurch. The reeds collapsed in front of me and I felt myself go under. With my right hand I struggled upward, trying to free my head from the tangle. It was as if a mattress was pressing me down. With all my strength I pushed with my left hand, then brought both arms up in a sweeping motion. The surface gave and I burst free, only to go under again. But I had gained another few metres and this time my hand found something solid. Panting with weakness, I rested there while my left foot searched for my cycle. It was second nature, now, to do that. Even if I had not depended on it for support, I would have used my last strength to drag my cycle with me. After 8,000-and-some miles and almost two years, our cycles were closer to us than our own skins. They were the structure of our journey, the framework of our lives. Without them we were mere crawling things. And then, too, we knew that practically speaking our journey would be over, our expedition aborted, if once we went on without them.

With my left foot I reached back and down, letting my head go under momentarily. By the way it felt I knew it was my bicycle. When I finally got it to the surface, it was as if I had given life back to a friend. Not for the first time, the thought flashed across my exhausted mind: how on earth would Susie have coped with all this? How could we possibly have contemplated bringing a girl on this expedition?

Susie Craig was an attractive, 19-year-old New Zealander. Originally she'd been part of the group. Two two-man teams: two tents, two stoves. It made sense. David was reluctant to include her, seemed ill at ease in her presence. Steve fancied his chances with her, I think, and was put off when I made her the other half of my team. As the expedition's leader, I had several reasons for wanting to include Susie. She was fit; she was eager to go, had the wherewithal; but most importantly, I thought, she would exert a civilizing influence over the rest of us. At the back of my mind was also the idea that our companionship might turn into something deeper, but that was not my primary consideration. I was 35, old enough to be her father, and I thought of myself in a protective role. How would it have worked out? How would she have managed in the Atrato? We did not have the chance to find out, for before we reached Punta Arenas, she was no longer one of us.

'She said she wasn't feeling well,' I told the others, steadying myself on the rail of the deck. So far on the voyage, she hadn't joined us once for our training periods.

'Bloody dagoes,' growled Steve.

The truth was that Susie preferred the company of the ship's crew to ours. Which didn't augur well for what was to come. So we called her in.

'I've decided to go on to Buenos Aires,' she coolly informed us.

'Isn't that a bit hard on us?' I said, hardly able to control my wrath.

'Oh, you'll get on,' she said. 'You don't need me.'

It was a question of commitment, I told her. Also, her parents had entrusted her to our care. She made a gesture of annoyance, as if the whole thing were really too boring to take seriously.

'Either you cable them or I will,' Steve said. She looked at David and me but we gave her no help.

'Oh, all right,' she said. And three days later we were released from our responsibilites.

It set the whole trip off to a bad start, however. Not only did we have to divide up all the gear, but we would now be forced to crowd into one two-man tent. Steve made no effort to hide his satisfaction. Looking back on it now, I can see that Susie's quitting was really his first victory. It was like the Australian slouch hat he wore the whole way up through South America. 'It would be like your sporting a bowler as you rounded up the sheep,' I told him. Of course, once he knew how I felt, he never took it off his head. 'It's an insult to the bike,' I informed him stiffly; there was a proper cap for cycling. Just as there was a proper way to set up the tent. But Steve never understood that. Each time his hat blew off, though, and he had to get off his bike and chase it, it gave me the most idiotic pleasure.

After ten days at sea we reached the Straits of Magellan. Beyond the oil tanks and gas cylinders, behind the tin roofs of the low stone buildings of Punta Arenas, was a ring of barren hills. Beyond them would be the pampas. To the west of the pampas were the Andes: the unknown. It was a thrilling prospect. On the passage in there had been mountains, patches of snow crowning their summits; stark cliffs falling to the water's edge, where fierce currents battled. It was a desolate country; reminiscent of the windswept parts of Newfoundland. Across the straits in Tierra del Fuego, a coastal plain led to a snow-capped chain of mountains. That was where we would be riding in the immediate future. What I couldn't get over was how strong the wind was. And how cold!

We disembarked, and bending into the gale, David and Steve and I wheeled our way over to the ferry. I'd heard about the winds in this land of the Hyperboreans, but I could not believe that what we were experiencing could possibly be regarded as typical. It was.

The wind swept us along toward the mountains of Tierra del Fuego as if we were flies. Our energies were divided between dodging boulders in the stream-bed road and trying to keep our heavily-loaded bikes from tipping over. Three hundred miles to the tip of South America – the Beagle Channel, that is – 'With this wind,' said Steve, 'we'll be there this afternoon.'

One week later we stood on the beach at the southernmost end of the Pan American Highway and shook hands on our vow to repeat this ritual on the banks of the Yukon, 18,000 miles away. And then we turned and faced the wind. It was as if a mighty hand were determined to push us off the edge of the continent. We had to lean into it; our tendons strained as we fought back up on to our seats and wobbled off toward the north. It was more like mountain climbing than cycling. The wind was blowing 50, 60, even 70 m.p.h. at times, and it was a tribute to our cycles and our condition that we were able to ride at all. It took us ten days to get back to Punta Arenas. If there had been a boat in the harbour going to New Zealand, I am sure Steve and David would have taken it.

Patagonia was worse than Tierra del Fuego: hundreds and hundreds of miles of pampas across which the wind swept in a steady roar. In the mountains one could find shelter, but here there were only the occasional lines of poplars, planted as wind-breaks by the few *estancia* owners who lived in this forlorn country. If we wanted to heat up some soup for lunch, we had to set up the tent.

All day and all night the wind howled. The tent, held down, miraculously, by boulders, was a nylon zip bag against which our confined bodies bulged and strained like so many Michelangelesque chicken wings. I had joked previously that thus packed together, one false move and we might find ourselves over a precipice; but the fact was that as Siamese triplets we were warmer and more comfortable than we would have been otherwise. What really got to us, however, was the unearstopperable roar. On the sea, the wail of the storm is a constant one can live with, for there are ups and downs. On the surface of the pampas, however, the sound is mind-racking. It is as if tendons and muscles and nerves were the rigging that bound the very body together, bone by spar-like bone. In the constant shrieking, one could hardly think.

Yet there was relief. Just before dawn the wind would suddenly stop – just as if someone had clicked it off. For one blessed hour there would be complete stillness. The ringing in our ears would slowly stop; and the crunch of tyre on gravel, the quiet hum of the wheels, the creak of strap against load, the clink of something in the pannier; all these delicious noises would fill our minds and we would speed on through the dawn and make as much time as we could before the wind built up again. The peak of the wind's ferocity always seemed to coincide with our setting up the tent.

We were 600 kilometres north of Punta Arenas, beset by the usual gale force winds. I was in the lead, ears ringing, listing 25 degrees to port; and keeping a watery eye open for a place to stop for lunch. We were pushing up a long grade, hugging the left as we always did so as to give us the extra width of the road should a blast knock us across, when I felt rather than heard a muffled explosion just behind me. I braked to a quick stop. A pick-up truck had swung sideways in the road. Just beyond it, lying very still, was David, the collar of his parka flapping wildly in the wind. I rushed to him and at the same instant the driver of the truck jumped out and Steve dashed up. The three of us converged on David's prone form.

'Don't move him!' I yelled. From the way he was lying I was sure his back was broken. I bent down to feel his pulse and just as I did his eyes opened; he turned his head slightly toward me and gave just the flicker of a smile. Thank God he was alive! Kneeling next to him, I ran my hands over his body. The cycle looked a tangled wreck, still caught under the truck's differential. There were skid marks in the road that looked to be a hundred feet long. How could he possibly have escaped? I thought, as I touched a spot in his thigh causing him to twist in pain. 'Don't move!' I yelled. 'Stay still!' Miraculously, nothing seemed to be broken. 'Space blanket!' I shouted, and Steve ran off. We should not move him, I knew, but neither could we leave him in the middle of the road. Carefully, we lifted him into the back of the truck. There was an *estancia* at the bottom of the grade, about two kilometres back. We would take him there, not try for the hospital more than 60 kilometres away. I sat with him, held him straight at the turns, banged on the window when they drove too fast, tried to instill some of my own strength into him with my eyes.

David turned out to be only very badly bruised. Some foul-smelling liniment, several days' rest, and he'd be ready to travel again. Thank God for that, I thought. Without David the rest of the trip would have been unthinkable.

'Did you hear that?' called out David. I lay still, every part of me listening. Had I been asleep? For I had heard nothing. Still nothing. I was immobile, not even breathing, trying to tune my ears beyond the hum of the mosquitoes. The throbbing in my leg was gone; my bites and rashes had disappeared. I was aware of only one thing: the noises of the night.

'What did it sound like?' said Steve, his voice strained with anxiety.

'Like a cow grazing.' A moment of silence.

'Ach! You been dreaming.'

My bottom was hanging in the water; I had tied my hammock to the only palms left for me and they'd bowed in the night. I was still soaked from the rain that had descended on us as we were setting things up. My stomach was a hard fist, and I continuously felt either ill or light-headed. Yet, for a moment, I could have laughed. A cow? In the wilds of the Atrato Swamp? Why not? All at once anything seemed possible. A whole herd of cows. Little white houses with thatched roofs; brick walls, stone where the rendering had fallen off. Daffodils.

And then, rending the night, there was the unmistakable, sputtering roar of an outboard. It grew louder, deafening, then faded away. We exploded with joy. Somewhere, very near, was the Atrato; where there was an Indian, drunk probably, tearing around in his outboard. Thank God for drunken Indians!

'Cheese,' moaned David. 'A nice, fat chunk of cheese, eh?'

'Cor,' laughed Steve. 'Like a cow, grazing.'

Sometime later in the night I awoke in a sweat of fear. In my dream I had been lying in a pool of water that was slowly filling with my own blood. Try as I would, I kept slipping under. I screamed out and woke David.

'Don't worry, mate. We'll be there in the morning.'

But by afternoon the next day we still had not found the river. After cutting in vain for an hour, Steve had climbed a tree. No sign of a river, but he spotted a hut some 500 metres away. We changed course, but after another hour we were still not there. Were we cutting up through a bend in the bank? That seemed the only possible explanation. Where was the hut? Were we to die in here after all – like Scott at the Antarctic – so near to food and life? But then I heard Steve shout, and some time later I too was gazing down upon the powerful surge of moving water. The Atrato! And the hut Steve had seen was in the village of Traversia!

Chapter Four

We stood on the bank, waving, and Steve raised his bike high over his head. Still the boat did not stop. It was a Colombian gunboat, and there was a white man wearing a pith helmet on the bridge looking at us through binoculars. 'Raise it higher,' shouted David, and Steve practically threw himself off the bank, pumping it up and down.

'You lads need any help?' There was a megaphone under the binoculars now.

'Yeeeeeees!' we shouted. But the boat did not even slow down.

'What the hell . . . ' cried Steve, as she sped past us. For a moment we were too stunned to move.

We even knew who he was. Back in Medellín we'd heard that the British Army Range-Rover Expeditionary Force was being aided by the Colombian Navy. Here it was, and the officer in command was Major John Blashford-Snell. Undoubtedly, our binoculared megaphoner was he. If we could have had the Major to ourselves for a few minutes just then, there would have been very little of him to return to his companions. Even in our condition, we would surely have been capable of instant dismemberment.

A canoe with an outboard motor on it followed closely behind the gunboat. It was towing a large rubber float on which perched a very battered-looking Land-Rover. 'So that's how they're doing it,' said David in disgust. But Steve was more interested in attracting the attention of someone on the further shore. Surely that dark spot across the river was a canoe – but was it heading for us? The vows we vowed, had the occupant decided to alter his course – but as it turned out we had no cause for alarm. The canoe got larger and larger. Finally a grinning Indian paddled up; and, one by one, we were ferried across to the village of Traversia.

There followed a period of the purest bliss. To sit on something solid! To allow one's rotted skin to scale off in the sun's pure rays! And, of course, there was food. We stepped out of the canoe into the aroma of baking bread.

The British Army wasn't at Traversia but ten kilometres upstream on the Cacarica, a tributary of the Rio Atrato. Actually, it was only a small advance party. The rest of the expedition was trailed out over some hundred miles. We borrowed a canoe a few days later and paid them a visit.

The welcome Major Blashford-Snell gave us was unexpectedly hearty, as if it had been he and not the Indians who had picked us up after all. Almost immediately he began telling us the details of his considerable accomplishment. 'You certainly can't claim to have driven the route,' I said, finally.

'No, of course not. How could we?' The plan was to get the Range-Rovers to the bridge eight kilometres this side of El Tigre and then drive them out. 'But let's be a bit patriotic, what? There's been a load of British taxpayers' money spent on this expedition and the least we can do is to claim success. On a technical basis, only, of course.' He paused for a moment. 'At least we did better than any previous vehicle expedition. Give us that.' But they hadn't done better than us and we knew it.

'I'll be damned if I want to back off,' I said to Steve later that day.

'Why should we?' he said. 'We did it.'

But would anyone believe us? Blashford-Snell, for instance, had said that he didn't know who we were when he saw us there on the bank. You could see that element of doubt on the faces of the soldiers. All right, we entered the swamp here; we walked through there; and we came out over here. Granted. But had we *really* done it? So, when George Busby, a photographer working for Canadian television attached to the British expedition, offered to film us in a bit of re-enactment, we jumped at the chance. And then he saw the track we'd cut, viewed with his own eyes our last camp; and we were not only included in the official expedition film, later to be seen on Canadian and British television, but we became heroes, of a sort, among the men we travelled with.

When the film was shown, by the way, there was no footage of British Range-Rovers being portaged on rubber floats around the Atrato Swamp. No. Here were the troops going into the swamp and there they were, in full dress, smartly stepping out of the jungle on a newly-constructed road, Range-Rovers taking up the rear.

When the film was shown in Canada, we were included and given proper credit; but in the British television version we were edited out. It was not generally recognized that we were the first to walk the Gap until much later.

John Richardson, the expedition's doctor, was treating my leg with some success, but we had to leave before it was healed. We reached Panama City two months later, though not without incident. In fact, had we not been befriended by the Forsters, a missionary couple who took us in when we got to Paya, at the end of the smugglers' track, my leg would certainly have had to be amputated. As it was, if David had not given me penicillin injections twice a day from that point on, I would never have survived. I felt eternally grateful to him.

About a week after our arrival in Panama, we found jobs working for a Salvation Army Major who ran a business on the side – exporting semi-precious gems – and he needed cutters. All he could pay was $1.25 an hour, but we jumped at it. After two weeks, however, I left, intending to take the opportunity of our extended stay there to write up our experiences. Nothing had prepared me for what was to happen next . . .

Chapter Five

'I've decided to stay on in Panama and continue to work for the Major,' said David late one evening over some wine.

'Is this some kind of joke?' I said.

'No, Ian. It's God's will. That's clear to me now.'

This was Steve's work, I knew, some trick to get me to react violently.

Steve added, 'And I'm going to enter a seminary. I'm flying back to New Zealand tomorrow.'

It is impossible to convey the complete confusion I felt on hearing these words. 'What about our tour?'

'That doesn't matter now,' said David. 'God wants me to stay here.'

So it was the Major's work. I wanted to shout out some blasphemy. Didn't he realize how completely he was being used by the Salvation Army man? And what about the oath we had taken?

'Why would God want you to stay with the Major?' I said. 'It's not as if you were doing missionary work.' For the next few hours I sat there, much of the time silent, while they tried to explain what it was exactly that had happened to them. Apparently, both David and Steve had been praying ever since we ran into trouble in the Atrato. 'It was a miracle that we got out of there,' said David. 'Don't you know that?' I said it certainly seemed like a miracle but that didn't mean it was one. 'Still the doubting Thomas!' said David turning away from me in disgust.

'Let me tell you, Ian,' said Steve, 'when we got to that high swamp grass, I didn't see any way we could get through. I called out to God. I said, "Show me! What should I do?" The answer was like a voice commanding me. I turned around and cut the other way, backwards. And that's what saved us.' There was such conviction in Steve's eyes that I couldn't bring myself to tell him what I thought.

It was about two in the morning by this time and all I wanted to do was get to bed. But David and Steve were raring to go. They'd kept it to themselves for so long that now they had to flood me with it.

The turning point was when I cut my leg and they realized that they might have to carry me out of there. 'Well, we knew we couldn't do that,' said David.

'I wasn't aware you'd planned to,' I said, sarcastically.

'Come on, Ian,' said David. 'You know we'd never have left you.'

'Do I?' I said, my voice trembling. 'I thought you made it pretty plain.'

'We had to save our strength,' said Steve.

'You never even spoke to me,' I burst out. 'You'd have left me for dead.' I was virtually crying now – sobbing, to be more exact – for myself – oh, how sorry I felt for my poor, wounded self; and out of frustration for not being able to penetrate their thickness. It was quite a while before I pulled myself together.

'If God did save you,' I said, sometime later, 'why wasn't it to finish the journey?' Neither Steve nor David would buy that one, but I went on. 'From here to Alaska could be a period of active testimony for you.' Perhaps there was sarcasm in my voice, or they simply heard me wrong. What I had in mind was the opportunities they would have at the speaking engagements we would be involved in. And I was being perfectly sincere. That I myself had no use for testimonial meetings, that I regarded my soul as a strictly private affair, was beside the point.

'Haven't you once felt His presence?' said David

almost imploring me. Suddenly I could see him saying that to some bum on the streets of Panama. That bony girl with the thin black hair and dandruff would play her guitar and there'd be a collection, and then David would walk over to some wino, some derelict who probably didn't even understand English, and smile and say to him, 'Are you saved?' Then I thought of the Forsters at Paya and the kindness I'd seen there, and for a moment I yearned to share their new-found faith.

God had been directing their lives ever since the Atrato, they said. They were in His hands and I could be too if only I would resign my petty human will. I was getting tired of it all. Finally I said, 'What about the money you owe me? How soon can you pay it back?'

'We don't owe you anything,' said Steve.

'You owe me $500 between you,' I said.

'We owe nothing in this world,' said Steve.

'Only if God finds a way,' added David coldly. They sat there eating bananas and drinking wine and had the gall to tell me they were now above material considerations. So I left them.

It was almost dawn. There had been several downpours in the night and the city was misty and ghostly-looking.

Crossing a square, I caught a glimpse of the hills we'd ridden down on our way here. It had just stopped raining then, too. The rain would soak us again before we got far, but in that brief space of time, speeding down that road, with the canal and the ships and the tin roofs and the concrete office buildings glistening softly in the evening light, life had seemed wonderfully full of promise. I was bursting with joy then. It was one of those great moments in my kind of life – this coming to the end of a difficult stage: downhill, the wind racing across your face, overworked muscles soon to rest; a sense of oneness with everything around you. And now it had come to this. I was alone, with hardly any money, abandoned by my companions.

Chapter Six

I had been on the road for thirty-three months – too long. One day I found myself cooking in my tent and discovered I had no memory of anything that had happened since lunch. I had ridden sixty miles that afternoon – over a pass and across infinite tundra, yet all I could remember was a brief conversation with a waitress at a roadside cafe.

'*You're sure that's all you want?*' She'd flashed a smile and a hip at me and then flounced out to the kitchen.

'*As a matter of fact . . .*'

'Idiot!' The pot of carrots and onions was overturned. A shoe I'd been drying had fallen on to it. I glared around me. Bread, margarine, peanut butter, a bit of mouldy cheese.

'*Eat your dinner, Ian.*' That nasal twang! I spun around. David's voice – I'd know it anywhere. Was I going bonkers?

'*You come a week ago, you wouldn't have made it,*' said another voice.

There had been a foot of snow in the pass. The United States border post was a mobile home; the door practically came off its hinges when the wind whipped it out of my hands.

'*Hibell? We've been wondering about you. Tell me, why do you fellows do it?*'

Why? Why indeed!

How I longed for this ordeal to be over; to see Mum and Dad again – to hear their voices, to sit around the table and tell them all about what I'd been through.

Yet each morning it was harder to get out of my sleeping bag; so cosy, so still. I tried to imagine what I would do in the way of a job when I got home, but I couldn't get past the home-coming. Bread. Tinned meat. Matches. Paraffin. Shoes need re-soling. *Hold on, Hibell. You'll be in Fairbanks tomorrow.* Only one hundred and sixty miles to Circle City – and that's the end of the road.

The plane trip. My parents. Then nothing – a blank wall. No more planning, no more psyching myself up for the day's run, no more biking. Good, my whole body cried out. No good, screamed my mind. Confusion. Terror.

Central America and Mexico had been full of experiences – mostly unpleasant ones. But the ride up through the States had been what you might call uneventful. Oh, there were moments, but mostly I biked from one party to another, being royally entertained – wined and dined and lionized and ogled – until I was fairly ready to join a monastery. Not that I'm complaining; it's just that by the time I got to Seattle, I was looking forward to being alone again.

The beauty of the landscape from Seattle to British Columbia is something I'll never forget – when I could see it through the rain. All those glistening mountains; at every turn, at each rise, a glorious vista. You fly along the road, unconscious half the time of your feet pedalling. The difficulties of the past are forgotten. You rise above the petty concerns that usually plague you; your view of the world becomes Olympian. Man is a spirit, a god, almost. His capacities are limitless. But then came the mosquitoes and more rain and a track that was so desolate and muddy that I couldn't have cared less what unspoiled mountains or glaciers or anything else were around. And then I was in Alaska, and the wind was freezing, and there were fifty miles between stops and an ugly, bumpy road through miles of nowhere to plod along.

I was taking the hill at top speed. Why? Because I *had* to get there that night. The thought of spending even one more night on the road was so loathsome I could not contemplate it. Slow down! My hands were frozen stiff and I could not claw the brakes shut. Swerving treacherously, I was startled by the face of the driver who loomed up and then passed me. I was the one who should have been afraid, not he. The cold had settled into me so deeply that I was no longer trembling. I heard the wind on my face, but I could not feel it. I sped on. Shine of ice in gravel. *Dodge it!* Follow the road. Rest at the bottom. My toes had no feeling – but I didn't care. Later I would deal with all that. In the meantime, take the curves tight, lean in. *Not too much!* Brake! *Brake!* The sleet whipped across my face like a steel net. The turn was a black hole down which I careened. The shoulder was a curb of granite; the valley a flat pan far below. If something had been coming just then . . . *Brake!* I shut my eyes.

There was nothing inside me to take the command. Numbed beyond fear, frozen past cold, I veered wildly, skidding sharply to the right. A car roared past me on the wrong side. Another. But what I was glaring at was Steve's face and the malicious smirk that spread over it just as he turned away. '*What yer doing? Trying to get me killed?*' Out of nowhere he'd come. Damn near forced me over the edge. Now he was gone. The trestle on the way to Machu Picchu. He had smirked just like that as he watched me creep along, terrified at the thought of meeting a train. The noise as it came nearer. Hanging there, how long could I stand the throbbing in my arms before I'd be shaken free? Once I looked down between the sleepers and almost fell. The stream was a tiny ribbon of white at the bottom of the green gorge.

My eyebrows were crusted with ice; I could barely see the road. Who was that behind me? David? How I wanted to turn, but I couldn't. There were two of me now: one bent over the wheels, riding; the other sitting back and looking around: a passenger. 'Come on!' I shouted. Was this the curve that we would not negotiate? Very likely. If not this then the next. What would it be like to fly out over the edge? I hoped we'd have a good long fall, not hit too soon. 'Watch it!' A spray of gravel. Almost over, but not quite. There was David. Or was it Steve? Just ahead. I fell in behind him, relieved.

I was looking up at a blue sky and wondering, absurdly, how there could be no clouds when it was raining. Above me was the front wheel of my bike. The road beyond was flat and straight; and in the distance, humped like the backs of camels, was a string of mountains. The wheel was still spinning and the 'rain' was the spatter of its wetness. But the sky was not blue, it was slate grey. And it *was* raining; sleeting, to be more precise. I rolled over on to my side, got to my knees, stood. I was shaking all over, but I was in one piece.

It was not till after dark the next day that I got there. A dog charged me as I came into town, but I did not even glance at it. I suppose it must have retreated, or fallen behind; but I would hardly have been surprised to find a piece of my leg missing. It had been rain or sleet the whole way and I was covered with mud. 'Welcome to Circle City,' read the sign. Beyond it was the Yukon River. I dropped my bike and staggered down to the water. The trip was over. But there was no sense of victory.

Chapter Seven

My face was pressed to the glass like a child's against the window-pane of a toy shop. Beneath me somewhere was the Thames, Westminster Bridge, the lights of Buckingham Palace. At dismal Heathrow, I assembled my bike and wheeled it out through the main entrance; then pedalled off into the dawn. I might have been any touring bloke, I thought, off early for a weekend ride. But I wasn't going far, not this time. Only to Stan's. He would undoubtedly be asleep, but he could sleep again some other time. I should have telephoned, but I wanted to surprise him. It didn't even occur to me that he might not be home.

'No milk today,' growled a voice. I knocked again, louder this time.

'Sorry, mate' I called out, in my best cockney. 'But the bill's got to be paid.'

A light. The shuffle of feet. It was all I could do to keep the lid on. The door was flung open.

'Let me have it, then,' a voice fumed.

'Have what?' I said, not raising my head.

'The bill,' he shouted. 'The lousy bill!'

'Oh,' I replied in my normal voice, peering up into his face. 'No charge.' Four counts and still he didn't react. Had he been out partying all night? He looked a bit thick in the head. 'Who is it, love?' I heard someone call. I'd forgotten he had a wife. 'Ian! My God, it's Ian!' burst out Stan. It was the old Stan all right. And what a welcome they gave me. We ate and talked and then ate some more. After ten years we had a lot to catch up on.

Around noon Stan called Brixham for me. I'd decided I wanted to surprise Mum and Dad, too. But he didn't get any answer. Funny, I thought. They never go anywhere. So he tried my brother's. It turned out Mum and Dad were at my aunt's in Hove. If I hurried I could make it there by dark. 'How's Mum?' I said as I left.

'Much the same as ever.'

'Dad?' But Stan didn't seem to hear.

The sun was setting when I knocked on my aunt's front door. My heart was thumping wildly and I had an awful feeling that I should have telephoned. My aunt opened the door and immediately put her finger to her lips. 'I'll get your mother,' she said, rather sternly. Something was wrong! But then I heard Mum's voice and I saw her running toward me. 'Ian! Is it really you?' She hugged me to her and wouldn't let me go, repeating the question again and again, as if she really didn't know. I couldn't get over how much she'd changed. Her hair was nearly white. Her voice, though, that was no different – as full of excitement, of life, as ever. And then, framed in the doorway, I saw Dad. He was an old man! All stooped over, shuffling along with a stick.

I called out, but he didn't seem to see me. 'Here. Over here.' I'd known, of course, that his eyesight had been failing, but I hadn't been prepared for this. I went up to him and he put his arms around me and held me. 'So it's you, Ian,' he kept saying. 'So, you're back.' He was half crying, too; his whole body trembling. We walked into the living-room.

I was wet-eyed by now, and so was mother; she was over-excited. It could lead to one of her migraines. My aunt came in from the kitchen, glanced at my mother, and gave me a withering look. Would I never learn? she seemed to say. I'd come unannounced, disturbed what was meant to be a quiet holiday, turned everything upside down.

Well, it was too much for me, too, I could have told her. I felt so shy with Mum and Dad. What I needed was just to sit down and look at them for a while. The word was out, though, and pretty soon the house was crowded with people. My cousins, Pat and Rodge, both had families now. As we talked, one of Pat's girls kept staring at me with big, saucer-like eyes. I was her famous uncle, whose letters were covered with stamps from all those far-off places: Marco Polo with tales to tell. Perhaps she was dreaming of doing something similar one day. I wondered whether I shouldn't warn her of the things she'd be giving up.

I had a terrible headache by now; what I needed more than anything was some fresh air – a little peace and quiet, some time to settle down and collect my thoughts. I'll ride to Maurice's house, I thought. My brother lived in Bristol, more or less on the way home. Mum and Dad had gone to bed, Mum with a sick headache as I'd feared. I made my excuses – I had to tell them I'd planned it that way all along; and finally I was gone, zipping along the cool road in the night. Bristol was too far, of course, but I rode for an hour anyway, thinking I'd give it a try.

'Swan's Tavern'. Its welcoming lights beckoned me in

and, feeling comfortably tired, I enquired after a room for the night.

'Sorry, sir. Only let rooms during the summer.'

'Somewhere to camp, then?' It was a cold night, coming on to rain. The disappointment must have shown for the barman relented.

A little while later I was seated comfortably in the tavern sipping a beer and munching away at a meat pie and some chips when a fellow came over and said, 'You the bloke with the bike?' I admitted I was.

'Off on a tour?'

'Just getting back.'

'Oh? From where?'

'Alaska.' The devil got into me, I suppose.

'Blimey,' he said, and called over some of his pals.

'What took you to Alaska?' someone said.

'Actually, I started off in South America. Tierra del Fuego, to be exact.' There were six or seven men around me by now.

'Bert. Fetch this bloke a drink, will you,' a man called out.

'Could have used a spot of that crossing the desert in Chile,' I said.

'Say, what's your name?' growled a suspicious-looking chap who obviously didn't believe me.

'Ian Hibell,' I informed him.

'I've heard of you,' said an old boy. 'You're the one slogged through all those marshes.'

'Much obliged,' I said and tossed back a Scotch that had found its way next to my elbow.

Pretty soon I was regaling the assembled multitude with an account of my visit to a Hollywood actress (admittedly not very well known) who had put me up at her hideaway in the hills for a delightful weekend.

'Blimey! Like a ruddy prince.'

'Bet he acted one, too.' Guffaws of appreciative laughter.

'Did you meet any head-hunters, any of those savages?'

'In Hollywood, you mean?' And the waves of laughter broke. It was like dropping stones down a well.

The hours passed and there were now about thirty hanging on to my every word. But by then my words were getting a bit blurred. 'We're keeping him up,' said one fellow, finally. He raised his mug. 'You're quite mad, you know, but here's to you, mate.' I tried to go on, but I couldn't. I wanted to tell them about the Atrato, about Blashford-Snell, about what it felt like to ride into those bitter winds in Patagonia. The images were clear in my mind, but they wouldn't form themselves into words. I was half led, half carried, up the stairs.

England. Dear old England. How good it was to be home.

Part 2

The Nor/Africa Tour

Second leg

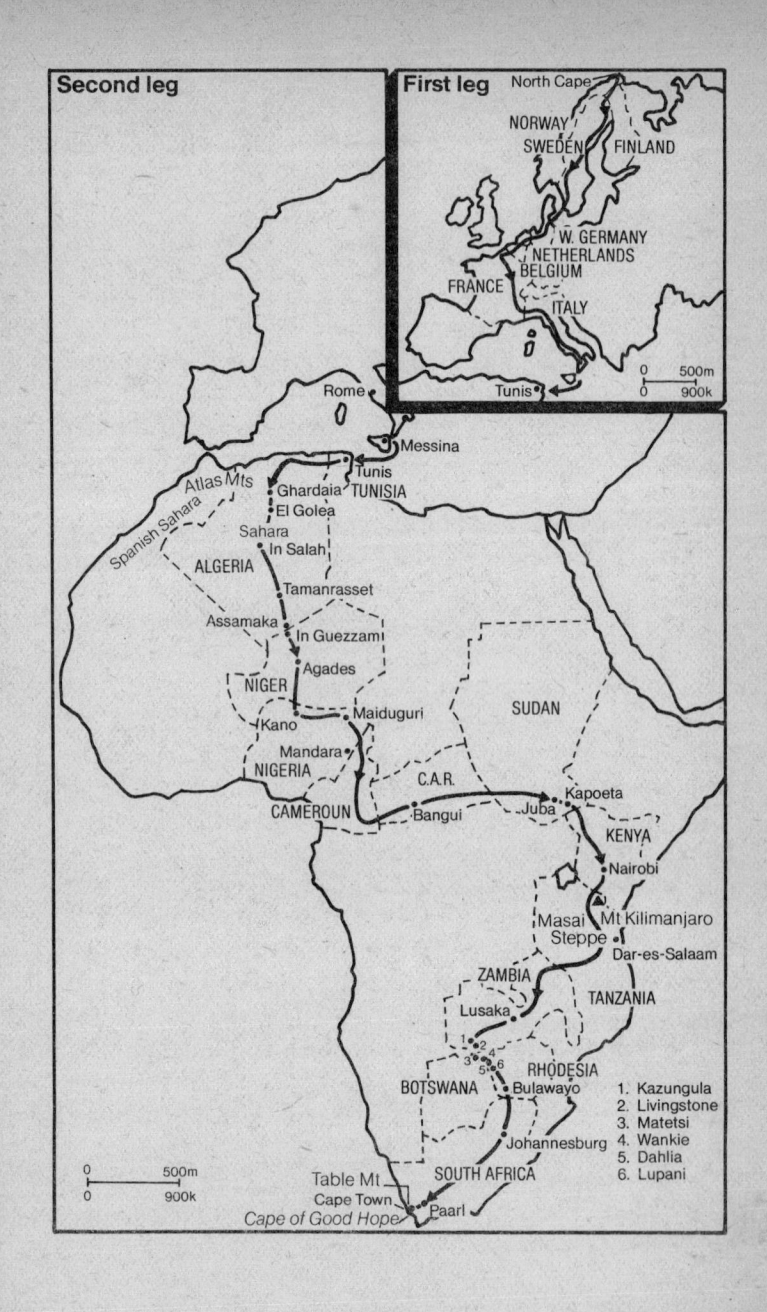

First leg

North Cape
NORWAY
SWEDEN
FINLAND
W. GERMANY
NETHERLANDS
BELGIUM
FRANCE
ITALY

0 500m
0 900k

Tunis

Rome
Messina
Atlas Mts
Ghardaia
Tunis
TUNISIA
El Golea
Spanish Sahara
Sahara
In Salah
ALGERIA
Tamanrasset
Assamaka
In Guezzam
Agades
NIGER
SUDAN
Kano
Maiduguri
Mandara
NIGERIA
C.A.R.
CAMEROUN
Bangui
Kapoeta
Juba
KENYA
Nairobi
Masai Mt Kilimanjaro
Steppe
Dar-es-Salaam
ZAMBIA
TANZANIA
Lusaka
1
4
3 2
5 6
RHODESIA
BOTSWANA Bulawayo
Johannesburg
0 500m
0 900k
Table Mt
SOUTH AFRICA
Cape Town
Cape of Good Hope Paarl

1. Kazungula
2. Livingstone
3. Matetsi
4. Wankie
5. Dahlia
6. Lupani

Chapter One

'The Sahara is the largest, as well as the most formidable, desert in the world. Temperatures climb to well over 130°; sandstorms cut passageways through the rock. Above all, there is the sense of desolation – not to be compared with anything else on earth.' Not much help for a cyclist there, I thought. Any more than in the other books I'd read. And the people I consulted were not much better. Some seemed to have derived their information from the pages of *Beau Geste*. One warned me to go well-armed 'because of the Tuaregs', an outlaw tribe that infested the area and would kill me on sight. I talked to travellers who claimed to have been through the Sahara, but when pressed turned out never even to have visited Africa. I heard everything: from how easy it was – you just followed the track – to a description in broken Italian which made the struggles across the dunes in *King Solomon's Mines* seem a Sunday afternoon promenade in comparison. Finally I found someone who was actually some help.

Tom Watson was an RAF squadron leader and had survived several expeditions into 'the great vastness', as it was called. Crossing the Sahara from north to south, as I was planning, would be very risky without some sort of support system, he told me. Air drops? Could I get time-expired parachutes from the RAF? I could. I already had a pilot. Colin McCulduff, of the Royal Automobile Club, had written a detailed book on African routes. I now contacted him.

'Seen you on television,' he said as we shook hands. He had a good memory – I'd been a guest on a programme called 'Globetrotters'.

Colin McCulduff was a very busy man. 'You're lucky,' he said. 'I don't generally assist potential disasters.' He screwed his face up as if daring me to contradict him. 'Been curious to meet you, actually.' Had I read his book? Well, never mind.

Our conversation was quite a long one.

'There's a good deal of soft sand. There'll definitely be places where you'll have to get off and push.'

'What about the track itself? Is it well marked?'

'There are oil drums and kilometre posts, but they get buried. If you're in a truck, you can climb up on the top and have a look around. In your case . . . ' He shook his head.

'And if you get off the track?'

'There's no track. Just the route across.'

What the track consisted of was a criss-cross of intertwining tyre treads that spread out in some places to a width of ten kilometres. Much of the area was composed of ancient, dry lake beds of the kind of landscape you see in American cowboy films. Drivers took what looked like the best route. They headed for distant mountains, went by compass. There were constant sandstorms, so the topography was always changing. What you took for a road often stopped at a pyramid of sand and the detour might take you many kilometres to the side.

'You wouldn't advise it, then?'

'You're something of a special case, Mr Hibell. I wouldn't presume to advise you.'

'You think it's possible?'

'I would have said the Atrato Swamp was impossible.'

'It almost was.'

'But you made it.'

'What about the soft sand?' I said. 'Are there dunes?'

'Some difficult stretches, but generally it won't be any worse than the beach.'

The beach? What was the man saying? He should be discouraging me, warning me off, and here he was practically egging me on. 'What about a companion? You wouldn't suggest I do it alone.'

'Is there someone you have in mind?'

I almost asked if he had anyone to recommend: a despised relative, perhaps.

I left the place, scared. Now I'd opened my big mouth, I was bound to have a crack at it; but what information had he actually given me? That there were no certain guideposts; no road, reliable or otherwise, for much of the way; and that I could count on lugging my cycle, and the 60 to 80 pounds I'd have to load on to it, over vast stretches of beach sand. How vast? Days – weeks in the crossing?

I had decided long before this that a companion was absolutely necessary, for no other reason than to share the considerable cost of whatever support we had to hire. What I needed was someone rich, strong, silent (or entertaining), who would cheerfully help bear the burdens; selflessly devote himself to leader as well as to expeditionary goal, and in sum, do everything in his power to make the whole thing enjoyable as well as a success. Since I knew no such person, I advertised.

Hector Brampton was 34 years old; he lived near me, and though not rich, he appeared strong. Ironically, he'd not seen the advertisement, but had dropped in to ask my advice about a trip which he was considering. Mine was just the sort of thing he had in mind, though. A challenge; he was eager for that. He was busy for the next few months, so meeting up in Algiers in January 1976 suited him admirably. When I told him that from Tamanrasset on, conditions were pretty much unknown, he said, 'Then we'll have to judge for ourselves, won't we?' His smile seemed to imply that nothing was ever as bad as people made out. Right away I liked his eagerness and his devil-may-care attitude. It was so opposite to my own.

Our first interview lasted nearly two hours. But at the end of it, I was quite satisfied. He seemed to understand what was called for. We discussed bicycle frames and even got down to how we would stow the water. However, to be on the safe side, I suggested that before we met again on the morrow, we each consider things in their worst light. If we were still game to go on then, we would immediately begin making the necessary arrangements. As soon after that as was practicable, I would return to Calais, where I had interrupted my ride down from Norway's North Cape to appear on television (on 'Blue Peter'); and from there I would cycle on through France and Italy to the tip of Sicily; then cross over to Tunis. Meanwhile, Hector would carry out the rest of our plans.

'Tamanrasset?' he said the next morning. 'Now just where is that?' I pointed it out to him again on the map. 'What's the problem? There's a road marked the whole way.' I had to explain the thing to him all over again. 'Well,' he said, 'if we can't go on, we'll just turn back.' There was something remarkably naïve but also attractive in this response, I thought. He was an innocent, I decided. How different from David or Steve. The fact that he didn't seem too bright struck me as a positive advantage.

I left for Calais that afternoon. I wouldn't be seeing Mum and Dad again until I returned, victoriously, from Cape Town. But we'd already made our farewells, I'd been home for eighteen months now (including the time I'd spent lecturing in the States) and they seemed to have accepted the fact that one day I would be pushing off again on another adventure. Mum was tearful, but she understood, and the idea of going to Cape Town was really an extension of Dad's and my old dreams.

I'd planned the Nor/Africa tour as far back as Alaska, actually. The idea of going from one end to the other of the Eastern Hemisphere after having done the Western, appealed strongly to my sense of balance. The Double End-to-End. From the North Cape to Cape Town was not as far as from the Beagle Channel to Circle City, but crossing the Sahara should prove adventure enough to make up for that.

Chapter Two

'You didn't bring a cape?'

'Don't believe in them.'

'What will you do when it rains?'

'See here, Ian. I'm not going to ride this bike in the rain. It cost too much.'

'What's this?' I said, holding up a sack.

'Goodies for the natives. Trinkets. That'll get us what we need.'

The things Hector had brought with him! How did he ever expect to get a quarter of that on his bike? Extra trousers, shoes.

'Where's the tinned beef?'

'I decided we could do without that. I'm a vegetarian, you know.'

For ten days I'd been sitting around Algiers waiting for Hector to arrive. Every day I would meet the boat from Marseilles. Every day I would inquire at the airport. The only word I'd had that he was even coming was from Mum, while I was still in Tunis. 'He says he'll turn up in due time. You're not to fret.' I'd sent him a cable from Tunis. No reply. Another from Algiers. When I asked him why he hadn't the common courtesy to inform me of his plans, he complained that cablegrams were too expensive. The room I'd booked at the hotel was too expensive also, he said. Why hadn't I been ready to go right off? We could have left from the dock.

Most maddening of all was the news that Beryl Burton – *the* Beryl Burton – had wanted to go with us and he'd put her off. 'Did you ever think of all the publicity we'd get?

We could have chartered a convoy of support vehicles.'

'I thought you didn't like publicity,' was all he said.

Where were the water containers? He hadn't brought them. Half the dehydrated food wasn't there. 'We can eat dates and oranges,' he said. I was white with rage.

'All right,' he shouted, suddenly. 'I'll take the boat back. The trip's off.' He started to pack the things up again.

'Just leave my share,' I said, in as icy a tone as I could manage.

'I'm taking back what I brought,' he stormed. 'You going to stop me?' I made a move toward him and he lunged for me. We fell on to the bed, punching and tearing at each other like wild men. 'Quit?' I said, finally, during one of our lulls. I think I had in mind letting him go, calling the whole thing off.

'All right. Stalemate. You're a tough little bugger,' he said cheerfully and got to his feet. 'What about some supper?' This was incredible. He was acting as if the whole thing had never happened.

On the way to the restaurant I told him about my problems in getting permission to cross the Algerian Sahara, caused by imminent war with Morocco over the Spanish Sahara. 'Fortunately, the story ends happily,' I said. 'The chief of the *Ministère des Affaires Etrangères* shrugged his shoulders, scrawled his signature across the petition, and said, "It's true, monsieur; all you British are quite mad!"'

We had no back-up team, no plan at all for dealing with the worst part of the desert. Before I left England, I'd tried to enlist the services of the Ministry of Defence. After all, they'd provided an Army crew for the 'Mad' Vicar of Manchester who'd pushed a sail-rigged Chinese wheelbarrow across the Sahara the previous year. 'We would be interested,' they replied, 'but we can no longer enter Algeria on a training expedition.' Though we had discussed his doing so, Hector had not succeeded in enlisting outside aid.

The best thing to do was to part ways for a while, I decided. As Hector was anxious to get off, and I still had some work to do on my bike, I suggested that he leave the next day and we meet in Ghardaïa, on the other side of the Atlas Mountains.

If he didn't show up, and frankly I didn't think he would, then I could consider our partnership off and set about the process of getting another companion.

'What's the game?' Hector said.

'No game. You want to go. You think you can take all that stuff. Well, then, go.' I even helped him pack.

The next morning it was raining. 'Cheerio, Hector. Have a good trip.' And I went off to the consulate to work on my bike. The consul was very friendly. He invited me to stay for lunch, and we ended up chattering most of the afternoon – and sipping drink after drink of his whisky. About four I wobbled back to the hotel through the rain, feeling very jovial in spite of the soaking, only to find that Hector was still there.

'What? You not gone? Thought you were in such a hurry.'

He was sitting on the bed, staring at the floor.

I tried to jolly him into telling me what had held him up, but I'd probably had too much whisky. Completely sober people don't care for those who've been lucky enough to escape their problems. At all events, I was more or less limp and when he gave me an exasperated push I fell to the floor, my head struck something sharp and blood started spurting out all over the place.

'What's happened? What are you doing?' screamed Hector backing away.

'Get me a towel, will you?' I said, trying to keep my voice calm.

'Oh, my God. When my people hear about this!'

I pulled out my handkerchief and clapped it over where I thought the gash was. 'No! No!' called Hector as I staggered out towards the wash-room. When I came back, I had the task of trying to calm him down. There was quite a lot of blood; I was cold sober by then, but he was still very upset.

I was so glad to get rid of him the next morning, I didn't mind the fact that he'd practically laid me out; though when I thought about it later, I regretted letting him take the tent. For two days I lay there, nursing my head; unable to read or even think very coherently; but on the third, I packed up my gear and very tentatively started out of town. I could ride, I discovered, as long as I didn't push myself too hard. I was still a bit dizzy, but my headaches had mostly disappeared. It was over 300 kilometres to Ghardaïa. In the mountains it was winter: snow squalls and ice on the road and piercing wind. If I hadn't brought my balaclava I'd have lost my ears. 'You were right, Ian,' Hector had written in a note he'd left for me at the consulate. 'I had to leave some of the gear.' He'd taken the trinkets but left the stove!

On the other side of the mountains it was spring. But I rode out across a landscape that was grey and bleak and rocky. Sand stung my legs and crept into my ears and nostrils. The wind pushed me out into a desert that was increasingly sandy and hot. On the third day I saw my first camel and on the fourth an oasis. When I finally reached Ghardaïa two days later, I was looking back at winter with nostalgia.

The restaurant I entered more closely resembled an opium den; the acrid smell of coffee competing ineffectively with the outside stench of mule droppings and urine. I tried not to tread on too many feet as I squeezed past a good many angry-looking Arabs, in quest of a table. I had a pounding headache, the coffee was like mud, and all there was to eat was a doughy, sickly-sweet bread. Why had I come here, I wondered? Hector had either gone on or had never arrived. I'd have to ride back to Algiers and begin again the search for a companion.

On my way out of the restaurant, however, I literally

bumped into him. He seemed overjoyed to see me. He'd found a hotel, and on the way there – how I was looking forward to a shower, clean sheets and room service – he gleefully recounted his adventures. Accidentally, he'd camped in a military zone and been escorted off the property in the middle of the night at the point of a gun. Monkeys had stolen bread right out of his hands. And he'd nearly been run down by a camel. I'd had no adventures. I was almost jealous. And I couldn't help responding to his good humour. Perhaps things would work out between us after all.

'Where's the room?' I said, practically choking from the smell.

'You're standing in it,' said Hector. 'The bed's over there, behind that curtain.' It was the wash-house atop the hotel, as disgusting and vile-smelling a place as I'd ever seen. But cheap. We should have been paid to stay there! There was the filthiest imaginable double mattress slung on a springless bedstead no more than a body's length from the 'toilet': no window, no bedclothes, undoubtedly an interesting variety of bugs. We were lucky to get it, Hector assured me. All the other rooms were taken.

Foul as it was I welcomed it, for in the past hour my whole body seemed to have undergone some sort of upheaval. Violent chills alternated with soaking sweats. My head was still throbbing and I discovered that I felt weak and dizzy.

'I'll lie down for a bit,' I said. And soon I was fitfully asleep.

When I woke up it was dark, so dark I could make out nothing whatever. I was too weak to rise, in any case. I lay there shivering, my brow wet with sweat, telling myself over and over again not to think, not to despair. Illness, however mysterious its origin, however severe, was something I'd always taken cat's cure for: sleep. Yet in this fetid hole, sleep seemed impossible. Hector? I called out in despair, my voice sounding weak and unnatural, but no one answered. I forced my eyes shut, concentrated on making my mind a blank. One, one-thousand; two, one-thousand three . . . By the time I reached forty-five I felt calmer. My heart no longer thumped. My shoulders ceased to tremble. Sixty-five, one-thousand. I held in my mind the image of the egg.

Curled up on a kind of floating nest, I could let my eyes explore the polished, concave inner surface of my stainless steel shell. Ten feet above me, the blunt point disappeared. There were no windows, no door, no opening of any kind. Yet it was neither too hot nor too cold. There was the vague sense of motion, as if I were in a vehicle of some kind, but no actual movement. It was as if nowhere were a place and I was in it. Most importantly, I was at peace. Any time I could get inside the egg, I was all right. The egg was my true home.

I thought of it as the room of my soul.

Someone was shaking me by the shoulder. Hector. It was dimly light out. 'How do you feel?' he said. 'You don't look so good.'

I blinked my eyes and groaned.

Sitting up exhausted me. I had a fierce earache as well as a throbbing head. My skin was painful to the touch. 'Think you'll be ready to go soon?'

'Not right away.'

'When, then?' I didn't answer. He shook me again by the shoulder, more roughly this time. 'Come on, old boy. Snap out of it. We've got to get out of here.' All I could manage was a groan.

I didn't notice him leaving but after it was quiet again I felt myself slipping away, slipping toward the egg. But I didn't get there. Instead, I wandered blindly through a storm of stinging sand; across vast plains in which vats of foul-looking, yellowish liquid steamed and bubbled, exuding the reek of sulphur. I climbed endless escarpments of grotesquely sculptured rock: petrified pterodactyls, monstrous hogs with staring holes for eyes, lizards with foul breath and coldy-gleaming skin. I staggered across seas of sand, head throbbing, scalp blistering. Finally I was forced to my knees. I crept on my belly. I tasted the ground and my mouth burned. My tongue filled my mouth until I thought I was going to choke.

Trembling all over, I crawled through the curtain and over to a low table on which stood a pitcher of water. I poured some of the blessed liquid into a bowl and sank my face into it. After drinking a dozen long, sweet draughts, I washed my neck, my face, my ears; then tipped the rest over my head. I dragged myself to the door and opened it. There sat Hector, staring out of the window. 'Decided to get up, did you?' he said. 'Ready to go?'

'Food,' I whispered. 'Get me something to eat.'

For a moment Hector just stared at me. 'All right,' he said, finally. I was leaning up against the wall, luxuriating in the light, listening to the street sounds below. After a little while Hector returned. He handed me a bowl of greasy-looking soup. I tried to drink it, but couldn't. 'Oh!' I groaned, nauseous now as well as dizzy.

'I'm leaving,' Hector said, taking the bowl. 'Obviously, you're not going to make it.'

'No. Please. A few more days.'

'Sorry. My mind's made up. Perhaps we'll see each other up ahead.'

He turned away from me.

'What are you doing now?'

'Packing my things. I'll leave you this,' he said.

It was the tube tent, utterly worthless as a noonday shelter.

'Don't take the other one. Or anything else!' I shouted. He simply smiled. We'd sent a huge kitbag of various items of equipment plus the ridge-tent to the edge of the central desert at Tamanrasset. Only the flysheet of the ridge-tent could provide proper shade from the sun.

After he left I crawled back to my mattress, weaker and

sicker than ever. What was the matter with me? The thought occurred to me that I might actually die in this dreadful place. Some time later I was jerked awake. It was the manager of the hotel; he looked both angry and worried.

'Your friend, he has left. Now I will have to charge you double.'

I don't think I really took in what he was saying.

'Food,' I said. 'Bring me some food.' An Arab boy brought black bread and coffee, some raisins and an orange I could not eat. When I woke again it was dark and my hair was soaked with sweat and I lay there, trembling, my head pounding, waiting for the light, not daring to close my eyes.

Later, by sheer will-power, I managed to get down the stairs and out into the street. Instinctively, I sought the square. Collapsed against a low wall, I closed my eyes. There was the smell of jasmine, the low hum of voices. I drifted away. Suspended in the air, floating, I became aware of the jar of one strident voice.

I opened my eyes.

'Say, buddy. What's the trouble?' Standing there in front of me was a cowboy: the tallest, strongest-looking, friendliest cowboy I'd ever seen. And with the largest hat. I blinked my eyes, but he didn't go away. 'Come on,' he said, holding out a hand. 'We're going to find a damn doctor for you. Sam, you take this feller's bike. Him and me're gettin' in this car.'

My saviour, who turned out to be from Arizona, got me a doctor, too, even though the emergency room was shut. Together with a terrified-looking orderly in a once white jacket, he carried me into a bare room equipped only with a green leatherette examination table. The doctor, who was French, conferred with the orderly, and in a moment I was lying on my stomach, my buttocks bared. 'Oh,' I cried, as the needle pierced my tender flesh. With a 'So long. Hope you make out all right,' my saviour departed.

Gratitude towards him was just being replaced by a delicious anticipation of being tucked into a clean hospital bed, when I heard the doctor say, 'Tomorrow. Back tomorrow.' No, no. He doesn't understand, I thought. He doesn't want to send me away from here. He can't. But he did. Handing me a packet of pills, he ushered me out into the street.

Where could I go? Even the filthy mattress was no longer mine, it transpired. Leaning heavily on my bicycle, I trudged toward the outskirts of town. At last I came to a wall. Beyond it was the desert. I propped up my cycle, laboriously set up the tube tent, and crawled inside.

Chapter Three

'*Ça va, monsieur?*' Not three feet away from mine was the face of an angel. Even upside down, she looked divinely concerned. She had a delicate nose; large, liquid eyes, like the proverbial gazelle's; close-cropped black hair, and a voice that suggested the tinkling of a mountain brook.

'*Je suis bien.*'

'Oh, you're English,' she said, laughing. 'Are you sure you're all right?'

'Yes, thank you,' I said, hesitatingly.

She shook her head, and her face disappeared. 'Jacques?' I heard her call. '*Viens! C'est un Anglais. Il a l'air malade.*' There was the sound of voices conferring in French, then another face appeared, upside down, at my tent door-hole. I unzipped myself and crawled out. 'Ian Hibell,' I said, extending a hand.

'Jacques,' the dark-haired, intense-looking Frenchman replied. 'And Maryvonne.'

'You *are* sick,' she said, looking at me once more in that wonderfully pitying way.

'I'm much better now,' I said. I was too weak to stand; so they sat down.

'Would you like some tea?' said Maryvonne. I smiled foolishly, and she poured me a steaming cupful from a thermos.

'We saw your bike,' Jacques said. 'You're on tour?'

'I was,' I said.

'Now I know where I've seen you,' burst in Maryvonne. '"British Cyclist Gears up for Ride to Cape Town".' I explained what had happened. 'Then you must come home with us. Until you are well.'

They were travellers themselves, off for a day's drive in the desert. Their house was Arab in design, but Western in décor: clean and cool, graceful arches, roof-top arbours and precious rugs. My room looked out over a valley of date palms swaying in the breeze. Cool thoughts! Cool shade!

Jacques was an architect, doing his national service here with the Algerian government. Their house was near the walled city of Beni-Isguen, into which no infidel may enter. We had arrived at the house by government car, some half an hour after my second trip to the emergency room. 'You are much recovered,' said the doctor, as if to congratulate me. I was pathetically weak; but my temperature was virtually normal. The gash on my head was mostly healed; and my ear infection no longer bothered me. It was hard to believe that only twenty-four hours earlier, I had been a homeless beggar longingly pressing my face up against the grave.

Maryvonne had two horses, and after I was sufficiently recovered, we took rides together into the desert. The mornings were still cool, the nights cold, and the horses would snort and paw at the sand, impatiently, as we watched the sun come up over that vast and silent landscape. We might explore an escarpment of wind-tunnelled stone, hidden among the apparently bare hills. Or we might go the other way, to where the dunes began.

Three hundred feet high, some of them, they billowed out across the landscape like waves, all the way to El Golea, 150 kilometres distant.

'The Grand Erg Occidental!' I declaimed. 'With a name like that, anything could happen!'

I stayed with Jacques and Maryvonne for two weeks. Towards the end of that time I reluctantly began making preparations for the trip ahead. What I had to do was find a way of carrying at least twelve litres of water, a four-day supply. It was not a question of the heat so much as the extreme lack of humidity. In the central Sahara, there is less moisture than in any other place on earth. Fingernails chip and flake off, clothes sparkle with static electricity. Just combing one's hair is enough to produce a minor electrical storm. There are no skeletons along this road. Corpses are instantly mummified. The sun is a vampire that sucks moisture up through the solid rock, leaving behind a tell-tale rime of salt. A bucket of water left in the open disappears in three days. The very pores of the skin serve as solar drinking straws. Even in winter, the longest a person can last without water in the desert is one day.

Out of camel-hide straps, Jacques and I constructed cradles for my bike that would hold four 3-litre water containers. Another litre and a half fitted into three feeding bottle cages. Granted a ridable track, I had the range of a medium-sized bomber. As I wobbled off down the road on a practice run, goats shied and an Arab who had been stretched out under an acacia tree jumped to his feet and ran away. I knew now what those blokes on the high wire felt like. It was as if someone had strapped a couple of fully-loaded barbells across the old machine. Keeping in mind a bear I had once seen riding a bicycle in the circus, I pressed on. If he could learn, so could I, I told myself. But for several hours, that was entirely a matter of faith.

The plastic water containers were easy to come by, on sale in the local *souk*. Jacques and Maryvonne themselves provided me with precious food.

'And you must take this,' said Maryvonne, handing me what looked like enough mosquito netting to supply a brigade. A *cheche*, it was called: eight feet of white muslin that wound round my cranium and made me look like Lawrence of Arabia – at least from the neck up.

'Where's the robe?' I said. 'And my spare camel?'

'You'll wish you had one,' said Jacques. 'Wait till you hit a dust-storm. Or one of those "dry rains".'

I took the tube tent, which I would send back to England from Tamanrasset, where, along with dehydrated food, extra tyres and some badly-needed spare spokes, I would be able to pick up the ridge-tent. At least, I hoped I would. With all water containers filled and an additional dead weight of carrots, onions, dates, and oranges, I cycled up out of that one verdant spot in all this wasteland of sand and gravel, wishing that the time had not come for me to be on my way. And what of Hector Brampton? Would I run into him? If I did, I would know what to do. I was no longer interested in a companion, unless I could find someone like Maryvonne. In Tamanrasset I would arrange with a truck going through to drop off supplies for me. That shouldn't be too difficult, Jacques had said. As I reached the crest of that barren hill and saw before me the seemingly endless expanse of rolling sand, those past two-and-a-half weeks disappeared. Hector Brampton and the miseries of the wash-room, Maryvonne and the delights of paradise: both were now unreal as I bent my head down to protect myself from the wind.

Chapter Four

From the Atlas mountains to Ghardaïa, the desert looked more like the final stages of some ancient ruin than it did anything natural. It was like riding through some vast demolition site, across a freshly-deposited glacial moraine, or along the rubbled streets of a bombed-out city. The terrain was uneven, terraced. Where there were vistas, there were alleys of vision. Along most of the route wind-pitted stone walls hemmed in the roadway on either side. Now, on the road to El Golea, 130 kilometres away, the landscape opened up. Following the conformations of what appeared to be an ancient river valley, the road skirted the dunes that piled up ever more impressively on the right. To the east and south the land flattened out in an even plain of hard-packed, rust-coloured gravel that was sprinkled, as if purposefully, with larger stones. Low bushes grew in widely-scattered clumps, and every so often an acacia tree offered its miserly shade. Within an hour, however, the road plunged into the dunes: up and down, up and down, like a ship making its way across the sea. The wind remained strong – perhaps 30 knots – and at each crest it peppered my flesh with sand; but, fortunately, it blew from the north and the west. I did not have to face it head-on. The worst thing was that there was no place to hide: no outcrop of rock, no tree, nothing but the troughs between crests, and one dipped through those as fast as possible because of the heat.

As the sun began to approach the horizon, the wind ceased. There was an intolerable moment when its glare threatened even more intensely; and then, at once, everything changed. The sky turned crimson. Out of complete stillness came a breath of cooler air. Standing at the top of a three-hundred-foot dune, I was surrounded by colour; held within the radiance of stained glass! Crimson, salmon-pink, green, yellow, then purple. Each a stage, each complete: as if each time the world were made anew. The shutter closed and it was night. I leaned back against my pack and stared up at the stars. Never had they seemed brighter or more intense. If I raised my arm, I could touch them. I lay there, bathed in light, cooled, it seemed, by pure brilliance. Not a sound, no living creature within miles. My weariness was gone. It was as if I could reach out and touch not only the stars but all those others who had ever passed this way before, all travellers everywhere; Man himself. The desert tingled with life – pure life. Man was a worshipper after all, I realized. His natural, unencumbered, most essential and perfect state was this: to live in exaltation, to communicate with essences.

The next day I left the dunes and started across a vast, flat plain. There was no vegetation at all; nothing but hard-packed gravel and an occasional patch of sand. At noon the sun was like fire; I sought, without success, the shadow of anything at all. Then, just as I began to wonder if El Golea had disappeared, the road suddenly dipped and ahead of me was a green valley: date palms, lawns, houses, a mosque. In a matter of minutes I was seated in a restaurant, enjoying a meal of goat's meat, bread, and a salad dripping with olive oil.

The ride from there to In Salah took three days. Almost immediately I ran into my first loose sand. It was blown straight across the road, and when I hit it I slithered and yawed as if on ice. Down I went, fortunately with no bad effects. Pushing my bike across, I recollected the words of the man in London at the Royal Automobile Club: 'no worse than the beach'. But this sand was as fine-grained as sugar. My wheels sank in half way to their hubs. Clearly it would be impossible to push through very much of it.

The wind blew harder as the day progressed. Every few miles I would have to dismount and half carry, half drag my monstrously heavy bike through a dune of sand. In one place the road detoured way to the left. I looked with awe at the top foot of a kilometre post sticking out of the sand, wondering what else was buried there. These were the drifting dunes. Here the desert was 'active'. In Salah, when I finally got there, was literally half-buried. There were buildings where only the roofs showed, palm trees with nothing visible but their crowns. A doomed city. The very walls built to contain the dunes helped to form them. They grew at a rate of ten metres a year. In other parts of the Sahara, their advance was more than twice that.

In Salah was a collection of red mud-brick buildings. No oasis, no cluster of palms, no tin roofs or automobiles. It was a city made out of the desert itself. But the people's robes were more brightly coloured than any I'd seen before. Their faces were deeply creased, worn, blackened by the sun; but they shone with vitality. Here was a city struggling with the desert for its survival, yet there were no beggars, no aimless wanderers wailing or mumbling incoherently. There was a martial air about the people. Even the children seemed warriors. And I heard more laughter here than in any other place I'd been. If the smells in the streets were abominable – no jasmine, no incense, to relieve them here – they were also crudely stimulating. Ironically, the sight of a man shovelling his way to his door filled me with hope, whereas the bulldozers clearing the road of sand outside El Golea had filled me with a sense of futility.

The first evening in In Salah, three Renaults pulled into town. With their racks of jerrycans, goatskin water-bags hanging from the windows, and sand ladders strapped to the side, I knew these were the people who could help me. It was a French/Swiss expedition and they were going through to Agadès, too. For the sum of four hundred pounds we came to an agreement. A great load was thus lifted from my mind. I could now go back to worrying about other concerns.

It was blisteringly hot here. What temperature the sand reached I do not know but my shoes felt like ovens. How much hotter would it have to get before they melted, I wondered? I had heard that dark-coloured rocks could reach boiling temperature, though this was still winter: the cool season. But I drew comfort from the fact that I was closing on Hector Brampton. He'd been seen walking, his bike apparently suffering from mechanical difficulties. I left for Arak the next morning, having arranged to meet the French/Swiss expedition there.

Eighty kilometres beyond In Salah, the paved road came to an end. The wind was blowing hard and for the first time I donned the Arab headgear Maryvonne had given me. It took some time to wrap it around, but when that was accomplished – with the aid of a pair of vastly amused Arabs – I found that my mummy wrappings produced an air-conditioning effect and also protected me from what was turning into a minor sandstorm. The track was pointed out to me by a grinning Arab. 'There?' I gestured. 'Where?' He continued to point across the empty plain. 'But there's nothing,' I said. The track was identifiable only by the fact that the rocky surface was polished by the passage of many years' worth of rubber wheels. It was bumpy, but possible to ride on. With all the sand blowing, however, it was difficult to keep it in view. To make matters worse, I could not find the compass. I must have mislaid it during my illness. How I cursed this loss now as I shoved off into the unknown.

By early afternoon the wind had increased to gale force. Grit blew into my eyes and I could barely see. The sand swirled around me, stinging my bare legs.

It was becoming dark as night. When I saw the burnt-out shell of a VW van lying on its side, I stopped, gratefully, and crawled inside. The wind grew stronger. It began to howl; higher and higher its pitch went. With each gust, each increased intensity of wind, the wreck would clatter and bang; and finally it began to rock. Trembling, it would almost right itself, then crash down again on to its side. A steady barrage of what sounded like small boulders rang against the metal. Though secure from the wind within my shell, I found myself gripping the springs of the seats to keep myself from being blown away. Most frightening of all was the darkness. What would I have done had I not chanced upon this protection? I had heard stories of travellers being trapped at the sides of cliffs for ten days at a time waiting out storms like this. I did not think I could bear ten more hours. And then suddenly the wind stopped. There was a choking heaviness to the air, and a silence as eerie as the previous caterwauling had been terrifying. It was dawn. At first I was simply aware that I could make out the shape of things inside the van. Then a pale green light began to penetrate the atmosphere. Gradually that turned to a brownish-yellow gloom, and the air started to clear. All at once the sun shone, and it became intolerably hot. I crawled out of the van and began to tear off the suffocating grave-clothes that bound my head. Then came the flies.

I had been pestered by these Saharan flies before. They are everywhere in Northern Africa, the natural product of a complete absence of sanitation. But never had I experienced them like this. It was as if the wind, having become exhausted, had given over its torturer's flail to its assistants. In this inhuman landscape, it seemed appropriate that the sun, the wind and the flies should be in cahoots. I mounted my bike and left as quickly as I could. I wrapped myself up again in my *cheche*, risking suffocation, but still the little beggars clung to me, finding snug hiding places in the folds. Fortunately they did not bite. Had they drawn my blood with the same zest they sought my moisture, I would not have lasted out the day. I tried to keep them out of my eyes, but I could not. Yet if but one of these flies touched the infected eyes of a victim of *tachiomi bacillus*, I would join the ranks of the blind, a group that contained a third of the population here. The children I had seen in the streets playing what I thought was blind man's bluff; I would end my days like them; but without their toughness, their humour, their acceptance that whatever came in life was the will of Allah.

In utter misery, having to stop and manoeuvre my bike through corridors of sand every few hundred metres, I sought, at noon, the practically non-existent shade of a thorn tree. Praying for wind – how fickle the mind of man – I saw approaching me, as if in a dream, two young boys. As they came up, one of them held out his hand. In it was a bag of dates. Gratefully I took a few. The other boy, meanwhile, had lowered a cloth sack to the ground and was unwrapping a small blue teapot with a most elegantly curved spout. While the first boy broke off dead branches from the thorn tree and proceeded to kindle a fire, the other filled the teapot with water from a pouch hidden away in the voluminous folds of his robe. Alakazam! In a matter of moments, the delicious fragrance of mint tea. Would I care for a glass? All this by gestures. I nodded my head eagerly, noticing that the fire had done double service: for the flies were gone. There was no town in sight, no tents on the horizon. I could almost believe that the two youths had stepped off a magic carpet. As I bade them farewell, I noticed a gentle wind had come up. Eased along by it across the plain, I cycled into Arak just as the sky took on its first crimson glow.

Chapter Five

It seemed a simple matter. The French/Swiss expedition would transport my four refilled water containers plus the dates, oranges and other food I'd purchased in In Salah to the 80-kilometre post on the other side of Arak. 'We'll put the stores in a tyre,' Claude said. I nodded. Blown-out tyres were a common roadside presence. But then a doubt crossed my mind.

'What if the kilometre post's not there?'

'Then we'll make a huge cross, out of rocks, and bury

them nearby.' And that's how we left it. All day I tried to conjure up visions of how the plan might go wrong. But I could not. If there was more than one tyre, I could explore them all. There were not likely to be many stone crosses lying around.

I passed the 79-kilometre point late in the afternoon and there, in the distance, was the 80-kilometre post. A tyre nearby. Excellent. I was already anticipating the delicious juiciness of a succulent orange. But there was nothing there. No matter, I thought. They must have put the supplies further off. I strolled fifty metres or so to the site of another discarded tyre. Nothing there either. Don't panic! I told myself. They must be somewhere around. I looked for a stone cross. Perhaps they'd taken double precautions. No stone cross. I rode back as far as the 79-kilometre post again, examining every tyre along the way as well as every spot where more than one stone lay next to another. Nothing. What to do? Tamanrasset was 320 kilometres away, and I had only two pints of water, a pound of dates, half a box of biscuits and a tin of sardines. I could, of course, ride back to Arak. I could also go on and hope for assistance from some vehicle. Four had been by today. Tomorrow there would certainly be more. I cursed Claude, the French, the Swiss, expeditions in general and this one in particular; and ate my sardines and biscuits. The next morning I finished off the dates and took a few gulps of water. With half a pint left, I rode on. All morning I pedalled as if on a treadmill, and with a strong sense that I should be riding the other way. No cars passed me. At noon I huddled in a sliver of shade beneath a rock. Why hadn't someone come? Where were all the travellers? I took a sip of water. Another. I had perhaps four sips left.

It was mid-afternoon. I lay, exhausted, under a thorn tree and stared into the distance. My tongue was swollen to the roof of my mouth. What was that? A swirl of dust. The rising heat of the desert shimmered before me like a wall of burnished steel. Yet in the midst of it there appeared to be a column of sand. Apathetically, I allowed my eyes to follow it. At the base of the column was a dot, a cube, enlarging itself before my eyes. A car disappeared in the shimmer, grew suddenly larger, then smaller. It certainly seemed to be a car. But would it pass this way? Would it vanish? Might it not turn around and go back? Or simply drive past? It continued to grow larger. It was coming straight at me. In a minute . . .

'Care for a beer?' I felt the ice-cold can burn my hand, smelled the hops. It tasted real enough. I spluttered; forcing myself to drink it more slowly. 'Another?' I accepted with gratitude. Karl Mueller was my Gunga Din. Before I had voice enough to thank him properly, an elderly man in khaki shorts jumped out of the car. '*Still!*' he bellowed. In his hands was a movie camera and he circled me, coming in and out; taking close ups of my face, the bicycle, the discarded beer can; all the while murmuring ecstatically in German. A film director? Was I going to get the leading role? Perhaps I could persuade him to follow me to Cape Town, feeding me cold beers through the window along the way.

Karl had an extra five litres of water, and he showered me as well with tinned food, packets of dried soup, and biscuits. Spooning peaches out of a tin with my fingers, I watched the Mueller team drive off toward Tamanrasset. No, it was not mirage, I assured myself, smacking my sticky lips.

From then on every car that passed stopped and offered me aid. There were six cars one day, eight the other. I could have done without the fellow who successfully begged water from me; but for the future, I decided, rather than put my faith in any two-nation expeditionary force, I would rely on the kindness of strangers.

When I pulled into the Paradise Camp Ground at Tamanrasset the first thing I saw were the three Renaults. Preparing myself to inflict violence, I strode up to Claude.

He greeted me heartily: '*Ian mon frère. Bonjour. Mais vous êtes formidable!*'

'I'll formidable you,' I growled. 'Where . . . *Where* did you leave those supplies?' I was positively fuming, clenching and unclenching my fists.

'You did not see ze cross?' he said, looking puzzled. 'Big. Like zees.' He stretched his arms to both sides.

'I wasn't looking for a cross,' I said, my voice fairly dripping with sarcasm. 'There was that 80-kilometre post, remember? The arrangement, I believe, was to leave things there.'

Looking a bit guilty, though nowhere near guilty enough, Claude explained: 'We thought better to leave everything in ze *camion*. You saw ze *camion?*'

'Of course,' I said. 'Near the 75-kilometre post.' An abandoned truck. I recalled it well. Emblazoned on its side were the words 'To Cape Town or Bust!' Underneath was scrawled 'We Bust'.

'You did not see ze cross?' There was no point in repeating myself. Coldly, I turned my back on him and strode away.

Tamanrasset, Algeria's southernmost town, lies at an elevation of 1,390 metres. Jagged cliffs of black rock, above which buzzards circle tirelessly, surround it. The air is clear, and cool. To the north rises Mt. Tahat, the 9,573-foot tip of a vast volcanic extrusion which extends more than 300 kilometres to the east and north. Here are the Blue Mountains, the secret stronghold of the Tuareg. Much of this vast area is unexplored; all of it is bare of vegetation. How I would have loved to make a detour into this exotic wilderness; but of course I could not.

I had been nervous about obtaining permission to continue my route. Vehicles were not allowed beyond this point except in convoy, I had been informed. So I was surprised and pleased to discover that this held true only in the summer months. Now, in early March, if the official was perplexed by my motive, he did not show it, for he stamped me through with hardly a glance.

But I could not leave without the precious ridge-tent and the spares. Where were they? Not at the camping ground, where they were supposed to be. Not anywhere in Tamanrasset as far as I could discover. After searching for three days, I was about to give up when I accidentally stumbled on news of them. I was at the *gendarmerie*. Apropos of nothing one of the police officers handed me a message – from Hector Brampton. I tore it open. 'I knew you'd never make it this far, Ian, so I sent everything back to In Salah. Except for the tent.'

I was closing the gap on Hector Brampton and he knew it. The hell with the tent, I thought. I had to catch up with Brampton.

The travellers at the camping ground were full of information about the track ahead – most of it contradictory, all of it depressing. I was coming to a great plain that extended deep into Niger: a distance of some 500 kilometres. This was the skull-splitting heart of the Sahara, the section we had most feared. But out there somewhere was Hector Brampton, which meant that there was no real question of my going back. I must confess, however, that considering what I was about to embark on made me give some thought to our respective sanities. Was he stronger, more capable than I had thought? Or was he as driven by fear as I was by hatred? And were we not both heading for our deaths? The only consolation I could offer myself was that I would undoubtedly find out before long.

The road curved ahead of me and slightly down. On both sides were low hills. At the tops of these were piles of fallen stone out of which jutted massive towers of rock. Layered vertically, these extrusions, some of them a good three hundred feet high, resembled gigantic banks of organ pipes, or the crenellations of impregnable castle walls. I knew that these formations were composed of the most ancient rock. Riding past them, it was as if I were witness to the evolution of the earth itself. Here were the shards of its first mountains. Through this valley a mighty river once ran. The plain I was coming to was once a torrid swamp. The whole Sahara had swarmed with animals, steamed with equatorial life. And I was riding through all that, beholding it, as if time were a road like any other and I its traveller, too. For three hours I coasted along blissfully. And then I reached the bottom, where the track turned to sand.

Dragging my bicycle through a substance that varied in texture from table salt to talcum powder, I staggered out on to the plain. The track disappeared, then appeared again. At the moment of doubt, another stake would rise, or one more abandoned wreck come into view. Behind me were the mountains. Ahead, some 300 kilometres away, was Niger. I trudged on. It was like walking on a seashore that had no sea. Only the endless flatness of sand. And the heat.

I had been pushing my bicycle for perhaps an hour when a military lorry drove up. A soldier stepped out. Did I need any water? Yes, please. Food? I gobbled down some iron-hard bread and a piece of goat's cheese. Did I know that the border post at In Guezzam was closed? For how long? No way of telling. The soldier got back into the truck. He smiled and drove off, leaving me to spell out the implications. What his news meant was that all vehicle travel between Tamanrasset and the Niger border would now cease. Which meant that my support was gone. Though I had sufficient food, perhaps, I could not hope to make three hundred kilometres on the water that soldier had given me.

Six litres. That would get me back to Tamanrasset. Certainly, it was foolhardy to go on. Yet the track could hardly be so bad the whole way. The border might be closed for weeks, or it might be opened up again today. At that very moment there could be a Land-Rover bearing down on me, packed with beer-drinking Germans . . . I decided to go on. Something would happen. Someone would come. Feeling like an ant that has just decided to cross a freeway, I tried to step out deliberately. At the back of my mind, however, I knew, as my Arab friends would have put it, that I was now in the hands of Allah.

Chapter Six

I would rise at dawn; walk ten kilometres; rest; walk another fifteen; then break for lunch, flat out, panting under my tiny spot of shade. There were few large rocks, no thorn trees. My tube tent was no flysheet, but it was all I had. Sometimes I could ride part of the way, more often not. That smudge ahead of me – was it a burnt-out vehicle? A rock? A camel? A truck full of beer? Whatever it was took half the day to reach. Sometimes it turned into a hill. Sometimes the hill was a tower in the air – the shimmering, green, watery paradise beneath it only a mirage that would flee before me like the dancing sand devils. I had feared these dusty dervishes that could knock a camel down and break its bones, but now I looked on them as friends: amiable ghosts that performed their arabesques just for me; harem girls whose only function was to entertain, to distract my mind.

Three days; 147 kilometres. The afternoons were interminable. Dullness overpowered me. I might have been walking on the moon; for all I knew the day's journey took ten years. Only at the ransom of all my other faculties could I put one foot out before the other. And even then I would collapse. Sitting on the sand, crouched over, I would count, very slowly, to one hundred. By that time my dizziness would have disappeared and I would get to my feet and stagger on. Without my *cheche* I would have perished the first day.

During the afternoon of the second day, a truck passed

me. Even though it did not stop, I was reassured. Another truck approached on the morning of the fourth day just in time to fill my water containers; and they gave me food as well. Dotting the route were cars and trucks that had long since succumbed to the forces of nature. Most were burnt out; all were stripped to their metal bones. At first I greeted them with joy, for they could offer me shade and protect me from sandstorms. I soon discovered, however, that the relief they provided from the sun was non-existent, and at night I had no need of protection, for the wind ceased. Useless to me, they became reminders of death instead. As I passed they seemed to reach out with mocking fingers of heat, as if to beckon me to them, entrap me within the finality of their own defeat.

Early on the morning of my eighth day, I saw my first camel train. Gently rocking from side to side, these noble and beautiful beasts – dromedaries, actually – streamed by me without so much as a glance from their liquid eyes. Not so their masters. Behind their veils, the blue-robed Tuaregs glared, their women and children clustered behind. These were the people I had been warned against. The women, unveiled, strong-featured, the glitter of gold in their smiles, looked even fiercer than the men. What were in those colourful burdens? Tents? Rugs? Slabs of salt? Silk? Or rifles and swords and plunder? Yet in this desert I was the oddity, not they. That same day I reached In Guezzam. Ushered into the fly-blown, baked clay settlement of a dozen buildings by a crowd of laughing boys, I was the circus come to town. I took on some sardines and water and that same afternoon plodded out into no-man's land, anxious to reach Niger before nightfall.

A permanent gushing spring was what awaited me at the military post of Assamaka, I was told. Palm trees, running water. That was the vision that led me on. And I could see it in the distance: a group of dots that remained exactly where they were no matter how fast I walked toward them. There was not one track but a thousand. Tyre marks criss-crossed the area; all searching for a firmer path. I joined the hunt, leaving the useless kilometre posts; switching from Dunlop to Firestone to Goodyear – to my brand: Michelin. How fresh the tracks? How far ahead of me my enemy? The sun slid behind the horizon in a final explosion of light: a red, molten sphere, visibly sinking. Half an orange, a quarter, a splay of golden peel. There was nothing to do but camp for the night.

A blustery wind came up with the dawn, and I hurried off, fearing a sandstorm. But where was the fort? There was no break in the flatness. Then, after half an hour of fighting the wind, there it was, rising above the horizon. I had camped in a shallow basin. The fort shimmered in the sun, elevated by its rays. By mid-morning I could see a line of trees and what looked like the reflection of water beneath them. To the east of that ran a wall. And then, instead of becoming more distinct, it became less so. It was as if I were walking backwards. An hour later, however, the haze in front of me froze into the clear outlines of buildings, date palms, a sentry.

'Welcome to Niger,' said an ebony soldier with an ivory smile. With a grip that could have cracked a coconut, he shook me by the hand and led me to his mud brick office. As he stamped my passport I looked through the window at my longed-for spring: a pipe with a dripping valve at the end of it; a trough. But it was water: an unending flow of sensual delight. The soldier grinned as I ran toward it, ripping my shirt off frantically, and I heard him guffaw as I plunged my head in. 'Ugh!' I spluttered. The reek of sulphur was almost unendurable, but a few seconds later I was splashing water over me again; oblivious, almost, to the smell. For the rest of the day I played happy hippo, or lolled in kingly comfort under the shade of a cluster of date palms, my royal garden. Such bliss could not last forever, though. Brampton, the soldier informed me, was only forty-eight hours ahead. I had to go on.

The sun was barely up as I scanned the track ahead for the familiar Michelin tread. There it was, meandering across the surface like a drunkard's. As the day reached its zenith, Brampton's tracks seemed to grow more and more wobbly. I imagined him staggering, as I was, falling; writhing about in the sizzling sand; his eyes rolling, his lips cracked and yellow.

And then I saw him, off to the side of the track, a speck in the distance. My pulse quickened. I pressed on with all possible speed. The sand shimmered in great sheets of molten gold as I staggered forward – panting, gasping for breath. The picture I held in my mind was of Brampton.

The huddled form ahead of me had not moved. Was he already dead? Where was his cycle? And then I realized that it was not Brampton at all but the mummified remains of a camel.

Later that day, the track became virtually impassable. Each yard, a full-blooded effort, left a deep furrow in the sand. I had to shift from one arm to the other to avoid pulling my shoulder out of its socket. There were 250 kilometre posts between here and In Tessoum, the first village. If conditions remained like this for long, there would be nothing for it but to throw my bike on the first truck and admit defeat: black, ignominious defeat. For three interminable days I ploughed the sand. In all that time not one vehicle passed me. I was down to my last two pints of water.

Towards evening, the landscape, which had stretched out around me like a great copper disc, began to undulate. There were hills of sand, waves on the horizon, and a few straggly bushes. Best of all the sand had become firmer. Not firm enough to ride on, but something I could push my bike over. Incapable of sleep, I decided to walk on. There was a sliver of moon. There were the stars. I walked all night, guiding myself by them.

Not till the pre-dawn light obliterated the stars did I lie

down to rest. Perhaps I had made thirty kilometres, but where was I? Had I drifted off the track during the night? As the light strengthened, my heart sank. The desert before me was bare of tracks. There were no kilometre posts in sight. The horizon itself had disappeared, concealed entirely in some places by low hills and bushes.

Leaving my bicycle behind me, I walked briskly towards the rising sun. Just one set of fresh wheel-marks would give me confidence. They would lead to others, those to the main track. My shoes left a reassuring trail in the sand, and I made rapid progress in the cool dawn. When I passed over the first stony area, where my imprint did not show, I took note of the lie of my shadow, broke a branch down with my hand, scraped an imprint on a chalky bit of stone. In half an hour, breathless, I came at last to some wheel-marks. I followed them over a slight rise, only to find that they disappeared into loose sand. I followed them the other way. They vanished again. I looked at them more closely, touched them with my fingers. They were as hard as rock. They had been here for years.

I retraced my footsteps to the stony patch of ground. There was that odd-shaped bush, that twisted bit of branch. Beyond it were my footsteps and I hurried on. The next patch of rocks was not so clear in my mind and after circling the area for perhaps five minutes, I decided that my footsteps must have been obliterated by the slight breeze. To save time I struck off to the west, confident that I must pick up my tracks soon. Instead of sand I came to more stony ground. Then, on the other side of a slight hollow, I saw a maze of animal tracks. Goats? Herdsmen? Sweating now, panting from the heat, I back-tracked and quartered the ground. In vain I searched for my own footprints. At last I sat down, completely bewildered. It was still early. I estimated it to be no later than 7 a.m. In another hour, though, it would be baking hot. I had read accounts of what happens to the human body in the last stages of dehydration. The skin takes on a parchment smoothness; one feels an agonizing, needle-pricking constriction as the blood is sucked to the surface; then it evaporates; residue clogs the veins, blocking the arteries; a light blazes in the eyes; and before death mercifully releases the sufferer, the mind is rent assunder in an inner apocalypse. I shivered. Nineteen hours was the absolute limit a human being could go without water in the desert. Without a covering for my head, I would not last till noon.

Why had I left my bicycle? Why hadn't I worn my *cheche?* Such a fool deserved to die.

But wait! I could walk north, back the way I'd come in the night; once outside the area of the bushes, I would turn west and pick up my own track. I jumped to my feet and practically ran across the sands. *Calm down, Hibell! Calm down! Proceed more slowly!* Keeping my shadow at right angles to my left side, I walked at a steady clip for perhaps an hour. I was still in the area of low bushes, but I decided I must have ploughed into these earlier in the night than I'd thought. Sweating heavily by this time, I decided to make the turn.

Trying not to panic, I tramped mechanically along searching for tracks. The sun was like a hot coal poised just above my head. My tongue grew thick and I could no longer swallow. I lost all consciousness of time. I knew now I was hopelessly lost. Soon my blood would begin to boil. And what if, by some miracle, I found my bicycle? A pint of water would only protract my torture. No, this was the end. I collapsed on to a patch of bare ground.

'God, help me!' I whispered. I knew I was as good as dead. Death was a fact. It was something I neither looked forward to, nor away from. I was simply waiting for it to come.

What prompted me to turn toward the sun, I do not know. I was not conscious of any noise. What I saw convinced me that I had already gone mad. Coming toward me was what looked like a figure out of the Bible –

seated on a donkey, clothed in blue. I shielded my eyes and squinted. Shimmering in the heat-haze, seemingly held aloft, just above the ground, the figure glided to a stop. It was as if he had stepped out of the sun itself. Its radiance was scattered all about him. When his shadow touched me, I looked up, expecting to be blinded by light. What I saw was the grinning, mischievous face of a young girl. She was examining me inquisitively from behind the folds of a dark blue robe. Behind her was a small boy. He was leading a donkey; she, a tiny white camel. Further away I could hear the faint bleating of goats.

I tried to speak but could not. Instead, I pointed to my swollen tongue. My Saharan elf held out a goatskin full of water. No drink has ever tasted so good. I thanked them – in French, then Arabic. But they gave no response. I leaned down and drew a bicycle in the sand. They looked at each other, and grinned. In all this wilderness, they knew where my cycle was. I tried to show them my appreciation, and praised God. And then the boy extended his hand, palm upward, in a familiar gesture. 'Money!' he demanded. He could have been a city street urchin. 'Money!' Yes, yes. But I had nothing with me. Later, when we reached the bicycle . . . Meanwhile, the girl examined my pockets. Deftly her fingers explored, emptying them of grit. Impatiently, the boy passed her the donkey's bridle and signalled me to follow him. It occurred to me as we hurried off that perhaps I was not the first European these children had come upon in the last few days.

With the directional instinct of the desert-born, the young Tuareg led me straight across the sands to where my bicycle and equipment lay, apparently intact. However, I had no sooner feasted my eyes upon this comforting scene, when three more young herdsmen appeared. In no time they had my belongings strewn all over the place. Grabbing a bag of sweets, I held it high over my head, shouting something vaguely threatening.

But one of the boys snatched the bag out of my hands; instantly, the others were on him; and then they were rolling over on the ground, tearing and snarling at each other like so many dogs fighting over a bone.

Crack! sounded the stick; a cry of pain followed. A stern, lean young man stood in front of me, his dark eyes fiercely commanding. He wore a blue *djellaba* and a black *cheche*; and at his waist was a huge, square-hafted sword. As I was wondering what to do next, he shoved out the imperious palm. Where was his share of the loot? If I didn't desire my head to be separated from the rest of me, I should find it – right away. Frantically, I rummaged through my things. A tube of suntan lotion? Just the thing. I handed it to him, hoping to convey by my smile that it was something of inestimable worth. He tasted it, spat, then looked at me with hatred. Hastily, I rubbed some on his arm and attempted to explain its use. He smelled the spot, and an evil smile spread over his face, as if he had just been introduced to some delightful perversion. He dabbed some on to his cheeks, put the tube into his robe, and gestured me to precede him. I complained that I needed water, that I was faint from the sun and lack of food. He pointed ahead of him to a low bluff in the distance. I tried to obey, hauled up my bicycle and slowly pressed on. But after a few agonizing steps, I stumbled and fell. He glared down at me, his fingers seemingly itching for his sword. What were the Tuareg rules of hospitality, I wondered? I hoped, at least, that they fed you before they slit your throat. With a rude jerk he grabbed my bicycle from me. With me hanging on to the handlebars, we plunged ahead, steering drunkenly through the bushes. Under the bluff was a large, open black tent. Beneath it a dozen fierce-looking fellow chieftains stood, hands poised on swords. What would they do to me once I reached them? But I was not to find out. Dizziness overcame me, and I sank to the ground.

Chapter Seven

Spluttering, gasping for breath, I stared up at the laughing, half-naked boy who had just thrown a bucket of water over my head. The bucket tipped again and I had just time to shut my eyes before once more being drenched. Around me I could hear the rise and fall of much laughter. Apparently I was the main attraction at a Saharan sideshow. I rubbed my eyes and staggered to my feet. Where were my assailants? All I could see was a motley group of decrepit old people; a well with a great number of naked children standing around it; and a large herd of goats. The boy poured the next bucket for the goats, who were butting each other for position around their cut-off steel-drum watering trough. The fierce tribesman who had brought me here was squatting by a rock a short distance away and staring blankly at the horizon. A woman emerged from the throng with a bowl in her hands. It was goat's milk – warm, delicious, frothy, sweet smelling, fresh. I smacked my lips, wiped my mouth with the back of my hand and thanked her. She offered me a flat loaf of bread, and then another bowl, filled with steaming couscous and succulent goat's meat.

Visions of foreign legionnaires being massacred by troups of camel-mounted Tuaregs faded into the background. However, I noticed a goodly portion of the assemblage was rummaging through my things. In fact, if I didn't get over there fast, I would soon be left naked. How to explain to a father whose child has a torn rag for a shirt that you have need of two? The best I could do was to divide up my things: half a bar of soap to her, a quarter of my coffee to him: three rolls of bandages to one person, all my salt to another. A small price to pay for restored life. When the distribution of goods was over, and the goats watered, they indicated it was time for me to leave. They had filled my water containers and now they pointed out the direction of the main track.

The following evening I saw my first vehicle in five days. The solitary track I was following had wallowed and detoured and been crossed by several others, but at last it had led to the main line of kilometre posts past which trundled a virtually steady stream of traffic. 'Hey, cobber? Could you use a coconut? How about a bar of chocolate?' At one point a bevy of American tourists bounced out of 'Safaris Unlimited', cameras clicking from all directions. A roll of pink toilet paper – a luxury, indeed – I accepted with pleasure. I could ride the track from time to time, now, but I didn't make much progress. Everybody who passed stopped for a chat. Still, I was happy to oblige. I would gladly have sat down with each of them and talked forever.

At Abangarit, a camel-trail junction, the road became firm and suddenly I found myself in an area of tall, waving grasses. The desert was losing its grip. There were thirty kilometres of pure sand to trudge through before I reached In Tessoum, but when I arrived there, for me the major challenge of the Sahara was over.

'Brampton? The gentleman on the bicycle? He left yesterday – for Niamey,' the red-fezzed, white-robed, mahogany giant – my welcoming committee – informed me. Niamey? That was five hundred kilometres to the west.

'Why was he going there?'

'He said that he was returning to England, that he had completed his stay.'

I clenched my hands in frustration. So, our *tour d'Afrique* was over. Revenge was not to be mine. Never mind. I would deal with Brampton when I got home.

The very last part was the worst. Five days out of Agadès, the road turned to moon dust. My cycle sank in to its hubs. It was like pushing through talcum powder. The effect on my nose, throat and lungs was devastating. I longed for a gas mask but took comfort in my *cheche* and choked on. The very best I could do was ten kilometres a day.

Fortunately, there were three wells placed just forty kilometres apart: Tadelaka, Tchin-Garagen and Elike. And then, at Elike the desert, *per se*, ended. The road beyond was a gravelled highway. In a matter of hours I was speeding along through a countryside that to my starved eyes looked positively tropical. Leaves replaced thorns, donkeys goats, and cars and mini bikes camels. At Zinder the highway became paved. And at the Nigerian border I saw my first flowing water in three months. There was a group of naked boys swimming in a stream just to the left of a bridge. I needed no encouragement to join them. When I went on again, dripping water, river weeds dangling from my hair, it was with a bicycle escort. Those not fortunate enough to own machines ran after us, shouting with delight. As I pulled away from the pack and crossed into Nigeria, I noted with pleasure that for the first time since leaving Europe, I was in a country where a bicycle was regarded as a valuable and desirable piece of locomotive equipment.

No matter what lay ahead, it was comforting to know that the tortures of the Sahara were behind me. As Ewart Grogan exclaimed about the Sahara, during his walk from Cairo to Cape Town: 'I have passed through it and now have no fears of the hereafter.'

Chapter Eight

The VIP 'residence' at the Raleigh Bicycle Industries plant at Kano is the Union Club of North Africa. For two weeks I stayed there as an honoured guest while I made my preparations for the next leg: the 3,000 kilometre ride to Nairobi. 'You can't go now,' an authoritatively pessimistic traveller informed me. 'Rainy season coming up, old boy. Even if it weren't,' he added, 'no way to get through Chad. Someone tossed a hand grenade at the President – or hadn't you heard?' I said I was planning to go via Cameroun and the Central African Republic. 'You take a picture of those bare-breasted beauties and you'll get an arrow in your backside,' he said. 'And as for the CAR, Bokassa will lock you up for sure, if he doesn't shoot you for a spy.' I was beginning to be irritated by this gleeful purveyor of doom, but I had to admit there was undoubtedly some truth in what he said. Anyone attempting to outdo a man like Idi Amin was certainly someone to stay away from, and I had heard of Emperor Bokassa's purges, his 50-motorbike cavalcade visits to unsuspecting villages. It was bad enough where we were. Caught between two coups, one never knew what might happen next. One day a blood-crazed mob would howl for the extradition of ex-President Gowan, then domiciled in Britain; the next a street would be renamed 'Murtalla Mohammed' in honour of their 'lost leader'.

'Well, then, dammit, I'll nip through Zaire and Uganda.'

'Zaire? Don't you know what the Belgians did there? And Uganda? Amin's a madman. Forget it and go home.'

I finally settled on the Cameroun, CAR, Sudan, North Kenya route, it being impossible to obtain visas for Zaire, Uganda, or Chad. What I should have done was to have my skin dyed black, as well. All the way through Nigeria I was berated with the ultimate local curse word: 'Baturi! Baturi!' I'd been called 'Gringo' in Central America, but the colour of my skin had never before been the subject of such loathing as here. Men as well as boys would jeer at me. If I rode too slowly through a village, I would not only be chased but pelted with rocks. Worst of all were the 'mami' wagons. These glorified taxis always had several men hanging on the running boards. Invariably one of them would shout at me as they went by, sometimes hurling a can or bottle. It got so that I would raise my left arm over my head defensively when I heard them coming. I thought several times of what that fellow in England had said about carrying a weapon. Not that it would have done me any good. You can't very well go bicycling through Africa shooting up the natives. So I perfected my vituperative abilities, risking being turned into missionary stew.

Two days later my stove blew up, and the floods came. I was approaching the Mandara Mountains on the border with Cameroun. When first the sky darkened, I dismissed it as the usual bluff, grateful for the fact that the equatorial sun was out of business for a while. When the first drops fell, I raised my arms to the rain god in thanksgiving. A few minutes later, I began to shiver from the cold. Pelted almost senseless by the hail-like drops, I sought the shelter of an overhanging rock, acutely conscious of the irony of my condition. How often had I prayed for just such a rain. For ten hours the deluge continued. My tent proved insufficient protection and my sleeping bag became a sort of floating sponge. I wondered how I could ever have neglected to appreciate the comfort of those dry, desert nights.

The next day, however, when the sun came out, I gazed in wonder at a world made new. Butterflies fluttered above the abandoned homes of fleas and chiggers. There was the most glorious, freshest smell. The countryside, which had been arid and scorched-looking, had suddenly blossomed. Tropical plants lined the roadside. The woods were filled with bird song. And before nightfall my eyes were feasting on the graceful forms of numerous topless maidens.

This was Cameroun, the Africa of my imagination. Though the natives carried machetes and bows and arrows, their greetings were as friendly as if I'd come loaded down with gifts. The very straw huts they lived in, with their beautifully stitched together, conical roofs, seemed to me dwellings fit for kings. With their soft voices, polite manners and natural dignity, these people were the 'noble savages' that in my childhood adventure books always seemed so much more attractive than the lords and ladies of 'civilized' countries. As we watched a group of nubile young girls passing by, hips swaying, heads gracefully balancing heavy urns, an old Catholic priest I had met murmured, 'Like a garden of tulips on the move!' It was a beautifully apt description.

The Central African Republic was a depressing country whose poverty was as naked as the bare earth compounds surrounding its crude huts. When I reached Bangui, I was told that my visa could not be extended and that I had ten days to get out of the country, after which I would be subject to arrest. Ten days to ride 1,200 kilometres? To reach the Sudan in that time on dirt roads with the rains coming would be an impossible feat. 'If I were you, I'd just go on,' the US consul advised me, Britain being no longer represented. 'The further you get away from the capital, the less they'll care.' All very well for him to say. I was used to the sort of harassment one got from petty officials in these countries . . .

'Open package!' If the post office official had said it politely or if it hadn't taken me so long to wrap it up, or if the day hadn't been so hot, I might just have smiled, wanly, and done as I was told.

'Never mind,' I said, having no means to rewrap it just then. 'I'll send it Air Express.' And I abruptly took my leave.

Three hours later I was back again. Air Express was going to charge me four times the already outrageous amount for postage. So I'd swallowed my pride and returned to stand at the end of an even longer queue. This time I was prepared – ingratiating, all smiles. I had the package open for him, the panniers and other equipment I had no more use for exposed and visibly clear of contraband. The man recognized me, of course, though he pretended not to. Barely glancing at what I showed him, he stamped the package through and I went over to a nearby table to wrap it up again. Then back to the end of the queue and another half-hour wait. I got to the window at last only to have it shut in my face. Closed for the day! Furious, I stalked out of the place and sought the sanctuary of the nearest bar.

'Come on, Ian. We'll drop you off,' Denise Manchester, one of the stalwarts of Kano's British colony, said to me the next morning. She and her husband, Ted, even insisted on waiting for me in their car.

I ran into the post office with my package. Good. Not much of a queue. Ah, ha! A different face behind the window. Advancing rapidly, I finally came to a position that was within his ken. Holding the package up to him, customs stamp forward, I said, in my politest tone, 'Like to mail this through, if you please.'

'Open package!' he bellowed. I couldn't believe my ears.

'But it's already been stamped,' I said.

'Open package!' he repeated.

A man can be pushed only so far. 'No,' I said, and turned on my heel.

As I reached the exit, I heard a commotion behind me. There was the man at the window, coming after me. Pushing through the door I ran to the car. 'Go on,' I yelled to the Manchesters. 'See you at the club.' They looked baffled. 'No sense involving you,' I shouted, and dashed off, followed by two policemen. About half way down the block one grabbed me, and I was ignominiously dragged back past the gaping mouths of the Manchesters.

As soon as we were inside the post office, one of them began to tear open my package, while the other restrained me. 'It's nothing but some cycle bags,' I shouted out. 'For the Harrogate Cycling Show!' Fat lot they cared. This was test equipment, designed by me. It might even be considered of some scientific value. The man in charge glanced at the opened package and told the police officer to give it back to me. 'Oh, no, you don't,' I fairly shouted and grabbed him by the shoulder. Dragging him back to the table, I shoved the bags into his face. 'You want to inspect my package? Well, you're jolly well going to inspect it then.' I held up each item. 'Satisfied?' I was trembling all over from anger. When we were done, I started to wrap up the package again. By this time, Denise and Ted were standing by, and Ted took it from me.

'Don't you bother about that, Ian,' he said, 'We'll mail it for you later.' I was planning to wrap it up then, but I didn't think I could trust myself to stand in that queue one more time. So I let Ted have it, gratefully, and they drove me to the club.

All the way through the CAR I was nervous about being arrested. In fact, it just about ruined my enjoyment of the ride – that and the daily rains. The only trouble I had, however, was right at the border. And I wouldn't have had that, probably, if I hadn't been seeing some missionary friends off from the tiny jungle air strip. Too near the police post – I was spotted! This time an officer checked my passport. Each page inspection took a year off my life, but for some reason he didn't notice any illegality.

So, late on the afternoon of September 15th, 1976, I cycled into the Sudan.

Chapter Nine

'Your passport, please,' said the police officer, stepping down from his truck.

'But I just showed it at the border,' I complained. It was pouring with rain and I didn't want to dig it out and get everything wet. So I tried reason on him. After all, they spoke English here. 'Do you think I parachuted in? I didn't cut my way through the bush, I can promise you that. Look at my bicycle plate. "Nor", Norway. Understand?'

'We had best do this at the station,' he said.

I'd handed him the passport by this time, but he hadn't even looked at it. So I said I'd ride to the post to save time. He didn't answer. Instead, he shoved his revolver into my stomach and gave a command. His men put their rifles down and thew my bike into the back of the truck. 'You too,' the officer said, gesturing with his pistol.

The ride to the police station – in the rain – took over two hours. I was cramped in between a pair of greasy oil drums. Every pot-hole threatened permanent damage to my spine. By the time we reached the station, I was prepared to eat humble pie. Standing before his desk, as erectly as possible, cape dripping, I waited for the police officer to go through my papers. He thumbed through them quickly and handed them to me with a smile. 'All in order,' he said. 'And, you see, we have saved you all that distance on your trip.'

'Saved me you have not,' I retorted and explained that I had to ride or push my bike every foot of the way.

'Well, then,' he said, smiling even more broadly, 'you can stay with us tonight and in the morning I will arrange for someone to take you back.'

I waited around all morning but there was no sign that anyone was going to help me. So, after lunch, I set off on my own. That evening, feeling angry at the loss of a day, I rode back past the police station, not intending to stop until I reached the next village. But I was hungry and when I found a suitable place to camp on the outskirts of the village, I changed my plans. I was rummaging around for dry wood, an almost impossible thing to find, when I noticed, with some annoyance, that three young men were approaching me. I glared at them, hoping that they would pass by, but instead of being put off they asked if they could be of any help.

One of them shinned up a tree and broke off some dead branches for me. The other two introduced themselves, and in a few minutes I was telling them all about my incident with the police officer and more or less apologizing for my rudeness. 'Old Katamba. You don't want to get in his way!' They laughed and laughed, but merrily, not at anyone's expense.

'Say,' said one called Dumyata, suddenly. 'Why don't you come home with us? We can prepare you a Sudanese meal.'

'Yes, please,' cried the others. I told them I would be delighted.

Dumyata, Macolo and Bostusi were school teachers. They had been educated in Uganda and were teaching here in the village school. 'Why Uganda?' I asked them.

'Idi. He offered us asylum.'

'While our fathers fought the Arabs.'

'But they let you back?'

'Oh, they made peace with us. They needed teachers.'

'But they tell us where to live.'

'Someday I will be in Fat Pisgah's place.' Much laughter.

By this time I was sitting on the floor of a crude hut, sipping a powerful, homemade 'whisky'; and Mocolo had just brought us two wooden platters. The first was filled with a bland, pasty mush – cassava, the unwholesome staple of the African's diet. The second was a slimy-looking dish I had never seen before. It resembled, both in texture and appearance, nothing so much as phlegm. Dumyata, seated to my left, put his hand gingerly into cassava (it was very hot), dipped the mess into the 'sauce', popped the morsel into his mouth, smacked his lips appreciatively, and passed the platters on to me. Controlling a retch, I took a small handful and, by dint of skimping on the 'sauce', managed to choke it down.

'Thank God for the whisky', I thought, taking a healthy slug. By the time the platters reached me again, I had gained sufficient self-control to take my modest helping without showing my distaste.

'Who is Fat Pisgah?' I said, at one point, more to distract myself from what I was doing than out of genuine curiosity. He was the headmaster, they told me; a stupid, backward-looking man; the tool of a government they had little faith in. He had been educated in Khartoum, if he could be said to be educated at all; he disapproved of whisky, and had no use for new ideas. 'He only cares that the children wear clothes.'

'And call him Mister.'

'He has never read a book.'

'Doesn't know who Queen Elizabeth is.'

'Or Prince Philip.'

'Or *Magna Carta*.'

'I think he is part Arab.'

They were curious about my trip, so after dinner I brought out my maps and went over the route with them. Dumyata longed to visit England. 'Why would you leave there?' he said. 'The home of Oxford and Cambridge.'

'I would attend the University of London,' said Macolo.

'I, too,' said Bostusi. 'For the economics.'

I couldn't explain to them the lure of travelling. You went to a place to get something, they reasoned. 'I must get some sleep,' I said finally. 'Tomorrow I'm off to Juba.' While we had been eating a fellow teacher named Subu had come in.

'You can't go there,' he said.

'Why not?'

'The road is sealed. No one may leave – because of the epidemic.' I looked around me. The others were nodding their heads.

'Why was I not told of this?' I demanded. No one answered. 'Did the police chief know about it when he brought me here?' Of course he did. I turned to the map. 'How can I go around,' I asked Subu. 'Up through here?'

'You may not leave at all,' he said, smiling. 'You must stay with us now.'

I spent most of the rest of the night pondering the situation. The next morning I heard the news on the radio: it was called the Green Monkey Epidemic. It had started some hundred kilometres south of there and was sweeping through Uganda, Zaire, and Eastern Nigeria. There were no accurate figures but many hundreds had already died in the Sudan alone. The village next to ours was infected. In a matter of days all the villagers would be dead. The only hope was to isolate the disease. Like a forest fire, it could last only as long as there was fuel.

By mid-morning there was a long line in front of the dispensary waiting to see the male nurse: the 'doctor' for the surrounding area. Some wore flowing orange robes, enormous gold earrings, and their hair, which was cropped very close, was deeply coloured with a red dye. These were Dinkas, Dumyata (who preferred to be called John) told me, a tribe related to the Masai, and, like them, cattle people. Their diet, which they appeared to thrive on, consisted entirely of milk and blood. They were a proud-looking people, taller and more finely-structured than the villagers; and in general they remained aloof, preferring the nomadic habits of the herdsman to the settled life of the farmer. They were part of a larger group who lived nearby, in the semi-arid plains just north of the village, plains that stretched right up to the Sahara.

'Why are they being inoculated?' I said. 'I thought there was no antitoxin?'

'He takes advantage of the situation to immunize them from other diseases,' John said. 'And who knows? Perhaps these shots will help.'

'Ouch!' I gasped. 'Look what he's doing to them!'

The nurse was jabbing the needle into their arms and then twisting it back and forth.

John laughed. 'If it doesn't hurt them, they don't think it's doing them any good.'

As we were leaving we ran into Katamba, the police officer.

'Ah, Mr Hibell. In good hands, I see.'

I glowered at the man.

'You are disturbed? Please tell me what is your trouble.'

'You brought me here. You knew about the disease.'

'Oh, but I did not know. None of us knew until yesterday.' He laughed, good-humouredly. 'Believe me Mr Hibell. I am as sorry as you are.'

'But I may never get out of here.'

'It may be that none of us will ever leave here. Consider that, Mr Hibell.' He laughed again, as if he'd just made a great joke.

'It is of no consequence,' said John later. '*Epwo m-baa pokin ingitin'got*. A Masai saying. It means "Everything must come to an end".'

Chapter Ten

Each time someone was reported sick, we lived in fear until we found out it was not the dreaded disease. A child was bitten by a viper and died, and all that I could think of was 'Not yet!' To make sure that no one left or entered the village, everyone watched everyone else. I could not attend to my own sanitary needs without John or Macolo or Bostusi following me. When I complained, John simply said, 'It is best.'

I could get no message to the outside world, and after two weeks I became very concerned about how my parents would be worrying. The last they had heard from me was in Bangui, some six weeks ago. I had hoped to get word to them at Bangassou, or Rafai. Now I was overdue in Juba by at least ten days. They knew I was in the danger zone. The worry I must be causing them increased my own.

Every morning we would gather to listen to the BBC for information about the epidemic. The government broadcast from Khartoum was in Arabic which no one could understand. Then one morning there was no news of it on the air. It had not disappeared. We knew that. It was all around. But other matters had eclipsed it and we heard no more about it. Was it getting closer or retreating? We did not know. No one came to our village, no one left it. We waited, in desperate anticipation, in utter tedium; in limbo.

In the early mornings, before the heat became too intolerable, I helped dig manioc tubers from the field, or pound them into powder. Cassava! How I despised that gooey mess – like a great, grey cow pat. And to eat it with one's hands from the communal platter! I felt like a child forced to consume his own mud pies.

There were five books in the village written in English: a geography textbook and four children's books. For much of those first two weeks I read and re-read them. Then I got the use of a room in the schoolhouse and some paper, and to an audience of window-peeking children I spent the next three weeks writing up my adventures. Recalling the horrors of the Sahara and my strong feelings about Hector Brampton was hardly my idea of amusement, but it did serve to pass the time. Meanwhile, the life of the village came to a halt: public meetings had been banned, the market closed. No weddings. No funerals. Nothing. As the days went by, and there was no apparent change in the situation, I began to think that if I didn't do something I might remain here forever. Perhaps everyone in the neighbouring villages had died. On the other hand, perhaps the epidemic had run its course and the rest of the world was merrily going about its business. So when Katamba told me that I was to be sent to a nearby village, whence I could almost certainly continue on my way, my immediate reaction was to rejoice. But then I had second thoughts. Why had Katamba been so secretive in his manner? Was he really doing this as a favour to me, or did he have something else in mind? Judging by his previous workings on my behalf, I might well end up in a viper pit. So I made a fuss. I told him I would register a complaint with his superior if he even broached the subject again. It was his duty to uphold the law, and here he was breaking it. Until the all clear sounded, I was staying here. I was surprised by his reaction. He simply nodded his head. 'As you wish, Mr Hibell.' I was back where I started.

At about this time, John told me that for my own safety I must lock myself in at night. 'Why?' I said. I had noticed that my friends' surveillance of me had intensified considerably. One of them seemed always to be at my side. Without answering, he told me to keep right away from the other villagers. 'But why? You must give me reasons.'

'Trust me,' he said. 'I am your friend.'

The very next day Katamba made an arrest. A man had been murdered. His assailant had crept into his hut and cut his throat, witnesses had said. Katamba had the suspect in the police station for 'questioning', and one could hear the man's cries throughout the village. Outside the station, there was much lively conversation and even laughter. When Katamba saw me at the edge of the crowd, he called out, 'Mr Hibell. Come here. I give you permission to watch.' I thanked him but demurred. What I wondered, though, was whether the murder had anything to do with John's mysterious protection of me.

One night about a week later, I was awakened by the sounds of scratching at the door. I lay there imagining some animal: a hyena, perhaps, a leopard, even. Then, in the dim light, I saw a hand reach over the top of the door. I suppressed a cry of alarm.

'Let me in,' whispered a soft, female voice. 'Quickly!'

'Who is it?' I called out.

This herd of Alpaca held us up for a while in the Peruvian Andes

Camping in the Grand Erg Occidental

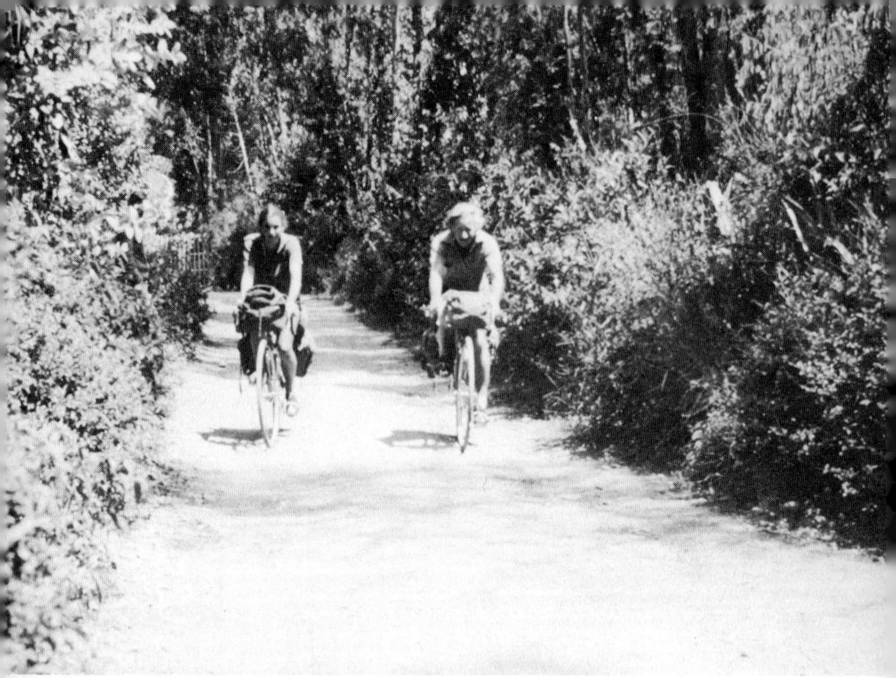

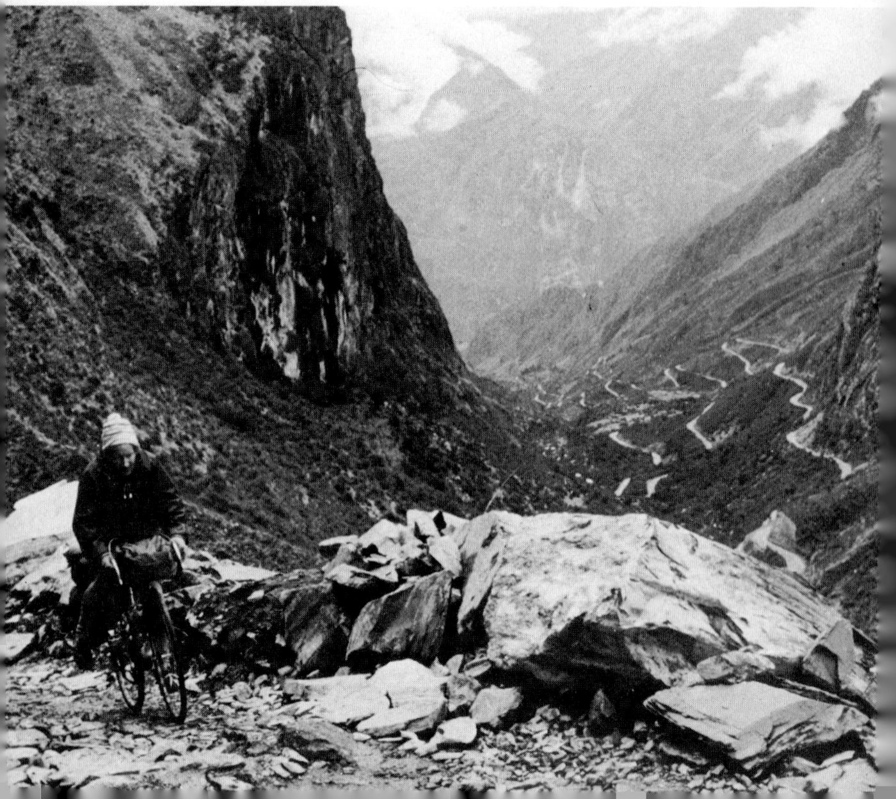

Jean chatting with local boys in Pomabamba, Peru
above left: Riding with Jean in the Urubamba River Gorge, on our way to Machu Picchu
below left: The return route from Machu Picchu

Crossing the Rio Manuripe

The tent, after an attack by army ants

'It's me,' she said, her voice pleading. 'Open the door.'

My friends were always insisting I needed a woman. 'What's your name?' I called out, stalling for time. 'What do you want?' No answer. Then grunting sounds and the thud of something heavy being moved. 'Who are you?' I repeated, growing apprehensive. Something crashed at the door. 'You've got somebody in there,' screamed a voice and the banging redoubled. 'Don't lie to me!'

There was wailing now, and then came a steady stream of the most vicious language I had ever heard. Some of the words and expressions I did not fully understand, but it was not difficult to make out their gist. The racket continued for perhaps ten minutes. All the time the door shook with massive blows. By now I was in quite a state. If the door gave way, the only implement I had with which to defend myself was a shoe; against such rage, that seemed hardly adequate. Surely half the village must be awake. What would they be thinking? If this was some sort of joke, it had gone too far.

The beatings and cries suddenly stopped and for a moment there was silence. Then I heard the sound of weeping: deep, emotional sobs. 'John! Please, John!' Then more tears.

'It's not John,' I called out. 'It's Ian.'

Screams. Yells. Violence as before. I was a liar, a traitor. Why was I not man enough to admit who I was and what I was doing? But I maintained a lofty silence. Half an hour later all noises ceased, and I lay down, eventually falling into a fitful sleep.

I was awakened by the sound of whispering: John's. Locking the door behind him, he stood pressed up against the wall, gesturing me to be silent. Finally, hearing nothing, he relaxed and sat down next to me.

My visitor was one of John's girl friends, he told me. When I didn't let her in, she took it for granted there was another girl inside. 'She thought I was you?' I said. 'What about my voice?'

'Who are you?' said John, mimicking me perfectly. John was furious with the girl, not for the disturbance she had made but for being jealous.

'What should she have done?' I asked.

'Gone home. Or found someone else.' Puzzling as the local customs were, I felt more inclined to congratulate myself for not having let her in.

I had been in the village for nine weeks when a young Dinka tribesman named Takli spent the evening with us. It started out convivially enough; but then, for no good reason that I could see, trouble began to brew. Perhaps it was the 'whisky'. Takli certainly had a superabundance of that. Whatever it was, he became violently angry with me, so much so that Macolo had to restrain him. He pointed at me from the other side of the room and kept repeating some word I didn't understand but which I gathered was distinctly unflattering. His eyes grew immense, and he began to shout. Finally, much to my embarrassment, Takli was escorted, rather unceremoniously, out into the night.

'What was all that about?' I said, not really expecting an answer.

'We had better tell him,' said John. Bostusi and Macolo nodded their heads. And so the tangle of mystery was finally unravelled.

It was the headmaster's doing. Fat Pisgah's. When I had first come to the village and gone to stay with his teachers instead of him, he had been jealous. I should have been shared around, he complained. There was also bitter political enmity between him and his teachers. He considered them radicals, who might easily be inveigled to resurrect the Anyanna and reactivate the 17 year-old civil war. So he spread the rumour that I was a spy, someone sent by the government to stir up local unrest. By the time John and the others heard about all this, the villagers were on Fat Pisgah's side. Several plots had already been initiated to kill me; ironically, one of these by the very man who was himself murdered. Just a few days before, Bostusi had seized somebody who was waiting for me with a knife just outside the nurse's quarters. I shuddered, remembering how angry I had been with him for treating the fellow so roughly. 'Katamba, then? Was he out to kill me, too?'

'No. He is your friend. He only wanted to get you away from the danger.'

'By sending me into the epidemic?'

'The village he had in mind was safe.' That was the first indication I had that communication with the outside world had been going on.

How I wished they had never told me. Often, in the night, I had heard drums beating. Now I was sure that they were beating for me. I could not sleep for nightmares. Awake, I would imagine arms protruding over every darkened beam. Each noise indicated some impending disaster. They could burn down the hut and lop off my head as I came stumbling out. I thought of a thousand instances that, in retrospect, clearly showed the deepest malevolence; of leers I had mistaken for smiles; of rude or inexplicable behaviour on the part of my three protectors that could have only meant that they were in the very process of saving my life. I could not sleep, yet I could not bear to remain awake. I implored John to stay with me. The three took turns, day and night. I hardly ever left the hut now, for I could not stand to see the villagers, knowing what I knew.

A few nights later, I was awakened from a fitful sleep by the sound of drums. They seemed not only louder than usual but nearer than ever before. 'John!' I hissed, but there was no reply. It was very dark, only a pale light coming under the eaves. I stumbled over to John's cot to wake him, but he was not there. 'John!' I called, suddenly terrified. Only the sound of the drums. I swept the room with my hands. Had they taken him or had he abandoned me of his own free will? I tried the door. It was locked.

The drums grew louder. Somewhere in the distance I heard a shot. Abruptly, the drums stopped. In the silence, there was the padding sound of running feet. An angry voice shouted out. Followed by others. Something heavy crashed to the ground. Then the sounds of a struggle from next door. I climbed on top of the table hoping to see something through the space under the eaves. I heard a cry, then more scuffling. The drums started up again, accelerating my already quickened heartbeat. 'John!' I shouted. 'Bostusi! Macolo!' Nothing. Only the wild beating of the drums.

Something struck the side of the building with a thud, and once again the drums abruptly stopped. In the deathly silence I could distinctly hear the sounds of my own rapid breathing, my pounding heart. An angry voice shouted something, very close by. There were other voices. And then there was a scratch at the door, a sudden shaft of light as it opened. It closed again, instantly, and I heard myself call out: 'John!'

'Shh! Be still! I've told them you are not here.'

Katamba had been the one to stop them, to save my life, John told me, later. A small group led by Takli, and fortified by 'whisky', had decided that only after I was dead would the threat of the epidemic be removed. Fat Pisgah was involved in some way, too. Thinking I was in the hut next door, they had stormed in. Furious, they demanded to know where I was hidden. I had been placed in jail for safe-keeping, they were told. They rushed off to get me. But Katamba would not let them in. The shot I had heard was his. So they had run back to Bostusi's and Macolo's hut. John had sneaked out as soon as he had heard the drums. It was he who had told them that there was no use in coming in here; that, as I was being held by Katamba, they had better wait till morning and then consult him about it.

All next day I stayed indoors. At noon John told me that Takli and his band had not been back to the police station, that he was pretty sure they had returned to their cattle. 'Whisky courage!' he said, and spat. It left me unrelieved, however. The next time they would muster a larger group.

'Hadn't you better tell Katamba?' I said. 'Perhaps I should be put in the jail?'

'He knows,' said John, and smiled. 'Katamba says it is better for you to be here.'

If I slept that next night, I was not aware of it. I had a weapon now, a panga, that Bostusi had given me. Part of the time I spent practising with that – until I felt quite capable of doing a job on a drunken Dinka if I was driven to defend myself. Towards morning, however, I must have slept, for I woke in terror from a nightmare in which Fat Pisgah was driving bamboo shoots under my nails.

The next two days were torture, though nothing happened. And then, as suddenly as it all began, it was over. A police truck – the first vehicle we had seen for ten weeks – drove into the village from the direction of Juba bringing us the good news. The epidemic was over! I was free to go.

In the general celebrations I was forgotten, and by the morning of the next day I was ready to leave. As the time for my departure drew nearer, however, I had begun to feel a deep sadness. These were my benefactors – my friends, my brothers. Even Katamba, stiff and formal as always, when he came to bid me adieu – and to inform me personally that he would be looking out for my safety until I was well away from the village – even he was moved to embrace me. Ten weeks. It had seemed an eternity. How could I leave John and Macolo and Bostusi after having been so intimate with them for so long? They made fun of my concerns, laughed at my worries, though they had tears in their eyes as well.

'I will visit you in England,' said John with the utmost seriousness. 'You may count on that.'

'I, too,' said Macolo.

'We will all be together again,' cried Bostusi, triumphantly.

But I knew otherwise. All I could do was hug each one, then turn quickly away.

Chapter Eleven

Fred and Ivy Taylor were cycling enthusiasts from England who had moved to Nairobi in 1952. They had written, offering me bed and board and general hospitality; and I had taken the liberty of forwarding my bicycle spares to them. Following my progress as reported in the cycling press, they were much concerned when they heard that I had disappeared in Southern Sudan. And when tales came to them of an Englishman who was pushing his bicycle through the jungle toward Juba, they knew at once not only who he was but, better still, what he needed. They put my spares on a missionary plane that flew regularly between Nairobi and Juba; and when I arrived at the headquarters of the Norwegian Church Relief, two days before Christmas, and Sven Knudsen handed me that package, it almost re-established my faith in Santa Claus.

The North Kenya Desert, through which I would have to travel, stretched down as far as the southern tip of Lake Rudolph. It was a 300-kilometre finger of the Sahara that protruded into the soft belly of Equatorial Africa. But it was not the heat, nor the absence of water, nor the lack of any track that made this project so unappealing. It was that this land belonged to the Turkana, one of the fiercest of all African tribes. A Turkana made a Fuzzy-Wuzzy look like teddy bear. Were the Turkana to rise up in revolt as the Kikuyu had, they would make the Mau Mau Rebellion look like a minor disturbance at a Sunday-school picnic. But that was an absurd comparison, for the

Turkana, especially the ones who occupied this northern section, were always in revolt. They lived by pillaging other tribes. The last group of missionaries that had been sent in to civilize them had been butchered. As proof of how dangerous they were, I was told that among them the bride price was not computed in cattle or goats, but in the heads of their enemies.

Yet these difficulties were purely theoretical, for there was no way to get to the North Kenya Desert. The road from Juba dipped down as far as Kapoeta and then went north towards the western tip of Ethiopia. From Kapoeta to the Kenya border was only a hundred kilometres as the crow flies, but at that point trackless mountains 3,000 metres high blocked the way. One would have to go around the mountains, past and partially through a vast swamp known as the Lotagipi; and almost as far as the Ethiopian border before turning south. There, at the head of the Great Rift Valley, the North Kenya Desert began.

There was another route to Nairobi: a smoothly-paved highway that ran through verdant valleys and along wooded hillsides; a route, in the words of the poet, 'where every prospect pleases'.

'And only man is vile'. That was the hitch. The highway ran through Uganda. And in any case, the border was closed.

In consequence of the difficulties outlined above, travellers going from Sudan to Kenya went by air or not at all. Actually, my choice was quite simple. Either I could hitch a lift aboard the missionary plane to Nairobi or sail up the Nile to Khartoum and fly back to England. Juba was literally and figuratively the end of the road.

I had been held up before in my travels. Yet never, it seemed, as absolutely as this. If I did manage to get to the North Kenya Desert, I was almost certain to be murdered by the first Turkana to come my way. And if, by some miracle, I escaped death by spear blow, there was a desert to cross that was physically even less suitable to cycling than the Sahara. I had thought that Lake Turkana (formerly Lake Rudolph) would provide a readily available source of water, but it was composed of brine. Like the Dead Sea, which it resembles in other respects, it is in the process of evaporating away. Another few million years and it will be a great salt pan, like the dry lakes in the northern Sahara. The 200-pound Nile perch, which still thrive in its shallow depths, will be flattened out into bas relief; the ferocious crocodiles rendered equally two dimensional.

There was another thing. The place was crawling with vipers. And yet, I thought, could not one put these matters in a more positive light? Salt water could be distilled. Vipers could be killed; even, if necessary, eaten, though I shuddered at the thought. And then Tipo Jago, Juba's police inspector, inadvertently came to my aid. He forbade me to go – by myself, that is. He insisted on providing me with a police escort. The 'shifta', or bandits, as the Turkana were called, had drifted up into the Sudan. 'It's my neck,' I said. 'But if you must protect it, you must.'

'It will be yours to protect at the border,' was his laconic reply, and he informed me that where I was going a camel would collapse from the heat, a goat would get sunstroke and a lizard would shrivel to nothing. However, I never received the police escort. At the last minute I was told I would have to go by myself. No explanation. No advice. Just permission to leave. So I went.

I reached Kapoeta four days later, having seen no one but a few spear-carrying, ostrich-feathered natives running along across a plain. I didn't stop to ask them who they were, or what they might be doing, nor did they me. Kapoeta consisted of little more than grass huts, a few dilapidated, tin-roofed buildings, a great amount of dust, and many cattle and goats; but I did receive some heartening information about the route ahead. Though there wasn't an established track, safari trucks did go through to the border and presumably beyond. They picked their way around the thorn bushes and the boulders, up and down the arid wastes of shale, along dried-up river beds, anywhere they could. They went in convoys, generally; armed convoys. They left no track. I would have to find my own way. But where others had gone, presumably I could go too. About the swamp, I also received reassurance: there wasn't any. At this time of the year it was as dry as bone. The bad news was that I would have to carry whatever water I required for the 250-kilometre trek.

I had thought my Gunga Din days were over. That's why I had sent back my desert equipment. Had I arrived ten weeks earlier, I would not have been able to go on because of the mud, but that did little to console me now. All I could do was curse my improvidence and attempt to create something out of the only available local material: the skins of goats. The result, after many failures, was bulky; it was awkward. It made me look like a decapitated hippo head with a bushel of grass in each cheek; but it held twelve litres. Even with the contents of my feeding bottles on the frame, this would not be enough to last the whole way; but there was a good chance, I was told, of finding left-over pools of rainwater among the rocks. There was even the possibility of rain itself, and there were rumours of wells. So off I wobbled. In the distance were the mountains that formed the Kenya border. Far to the east I could see where they began to lose their height. Though there was no track, I could hardly lose my way.

On three occasions I found pools of stagnant water, scummy with algae and malodorous in the extreme, but life to me. Once it rained, and I was able to collect just over a litre; but as for springs, or water-holes, or anything resembling wells, there was none. The only people I met along this first leg were a small tribe of Dinka herdsmen. They were digging in a dry stream-bed with their sticks.

We dug together for a while, until eventually we were rewarded with a few cupfuls of muddy water. They were silent and depressed. 'Kenya?' I said, pointing, and they nodded. But there was nothing in their manner to suggest that it was a place worth going to.

I came at last to a sandy river-bed. By my calculations I would be in Kenya once I crossed it. I started to climb the long slope that was the last remnant, I supposed, of the mountain chain I had been skirting. Suddenly a figure in a flowing, faded orange robe, brandishing a spear, stepped out into my path. Behind him another. Gold hoops the size of necklaces dangled from their ears. Their glowering faces were hideously scarred. I froze, rooted to the spot in terror. These were the Turkana. In a moment I would know what it felt like to be skewered through the chest on a spear.

Chapter Twelve

As the savage approached, his face broke into a smile. He dropped his spear and held out both his hands. '*Karibu*,' he said. Nervously I extended my right hand, which he grabbed in both his own, pulling me towards him in an embrace. Meanwhile, his friend had seized my cycle and was busily pushing it up the hill. 'No. No.' I called out, running after him. 'Not allowed!' He kept on pushing. I got hold of the handlebars, but by this time the other savage had taken up the rear; and the result was that the three of us were speeding up the hill as if it weren't there. It was a long hill, a good two kilometres. Grunting in unison, we pushed our way to within sight of the top. All at once, one of them let go. He stood there for a moment as we went on past him and then bounded off, gazelle-like, down the slope. I glanced back at his friend, but he was still puffing at my rear. The smile he gave me looked reassuring, as if to say that, though his companion had proved a slacker, I could count on him to finish the job.

We reached the top, and I was just making plans for a well-deserved rest and a bit of sign language chit-chat when the bike was wrenched from my hands, and there was my faithful helper in the process of making off with my sweater and my jacket. So that was the plan, eh? The buggers, I thought, as I watched my erstwhile good Samaritan leap down the hill with my precious belongings. 'Stop, thief!' I yelled, swerving around at the same time. He disappeared over a rise and I leapt on the bike and set off in hot pursuit.

The track we'd been following was rough in the extreme and at the very first drop, I almost lost control. Skidding, cursing, shouting, I careened down the slope up which we had so laboriously climbed, until, at the very bottom, I caught up, not with the thief, but his companion. Just as I was about to lay hands on him, the true thief burst through the bushes beside us. 'You scoundrel!' I bellowed. 'Give me back my things!' He stopped, seemingly stunned. I explained that if he didn't give me back my sweater and jacket I would find a policeman. He would pay for this. I would see to it that his cattle were taken from him. His wives would not be safe. Nor his children. Finally, at a gesture from his companion, he sheepishly handed me my jacket. 'Not so fast!' I cried as he started to sidle off. 'The sweater, too.' He gazed at me imploringly. He didn't have it. I knew very well he did and told him so in no uncertain terms. He shook his head and got down on his knees. He did not have my sweater, he said, and rubbed his forehead into the dust at my feet. I was unjustly accusing him. There was no mistaking the hurt look in his eyes.

'Where is it then?' I shouted. 'Who has it?' As if he understood my every word, he pointed to his friend. Until then the other fellow had been squatting on the ground, observing the scene with some amusement. At these words, however, he jumped to his feet and made ready to run. Grabbing him by the arm, I demanded that he give me back what was mine. In a violent, twisting motion, he broke my grip, but he did not run. He stepped backward. I followed him, gripping my cycle as if it were a weapon. With a sudden sweep, he pulled aside his robe. A knife, I thought. But no, there was my sweater tied around his waist! Deftly, he undid the knot. Looking chagrined, he allowed his robe to fall back down over his nakedness. And then, without further ado, the two trotted off. My sweater lay in a heap in the dust. I picked it up, stuffed it and the jacket back into my clothes bag. In the distance I could see my two Turkana warriors leaping across the desolate countryside. Beyond them was a herd of cattle. The glint of a spearhead indicated the presence of yet another herdsman/thief. Undoubtedly there were more.

It was not until I reached the top of the hill again that my anger cooled sufficiently for me to give my situation some objective thought. I had better make preparations to defend myself, I decided. While I was riding I felt relatively safe. This was open country, with few, if any, places for a person to hide. The track was uneven, to put it mildly, but from here it would have to be mostly down hill. Yet when I looked out over the rolling, barren countryside beneath me to where Lake Turkana glistened in the distance, my will faltered. If only I were climbing out on to the Kenyan plains instead of descending into this hell-hole. The Great Rift Valley is one of the most ancient places on earth, the home of the great Leakey digs, where evidence of the first man was unearthed. Yet all I could think of were snakes and the Turkana and the ordeal by thirst that lay ahead of me. In addition to these horrors was the wind: searing, choking; as if I had opened the door to a furnace and were now about to ride in. The immediate problem, however, was to find a safe place to camp for the night. The Turkana, I was pretty sure, would follow me. In the daytime, I could outride them, but what

I needed at night was a fortress, a place to hide.

I came to a series of small escarpments. I explored the area thoroughly, but found nothing suitable. Then, just as I was about to give up, I came to the perfect spot: a fissure just wide enough for me to slide through that opened up into a very small, topless cave. There was just room for me to lie down, no way anyone else could enter except as I had. There were no snakes, nothing but sheer walls of rock stretching up into the sky. So as to be warned in case anyone discovered me, I booby-trapped the area; tying mess cans to bits of rock and branches and spreading pieces of thorn bush about outside. Not wanting to give away my position by lighting a fire, I ate a dinner of stale bread and tuna fish, gulped down some of my precious water, and prepared for sleep.

But my mind was far too active for that. All afternoon I had been trying to puzzle out the behaviour of the Turkana. Why had they run away when they could so easily have demolished me? In future, if I gave them things would they leave me alone, perhaps even help me, as the Tuareg had? Certainly that was a crew whose reputation for violence outdid their performance. These savages were mostly cowards, I decided. Confront them and they back down. Naturally, they would parboil a couple of mild-mannered missionaries. Dumyata (John) had told me a story about himself and a lion that seemed to illustrate the point. I wondered if memory of that story had not, in fact, inspired my own reaction.

When John was a young boy there was a prize goat named Ebenezer in the village which it was his job to guard. Waking from a brief, illicit nap, he had heard the goat's cries and rushed over to find a lion attacking it. Without thinking he grabbed Ebenezer's two back legs and pulled with all his might. The lion had the goat by the neck and was pulling the other way and growling. John kept tugging, guilt for having fallen asleep momentarily outweighing his fear. And then, suddenly, the lion released his grip and bounded off. Ebenezer was dead, but the lion did not come back. Later on one of the village elders explained the lion's behaviour to him. 'A lion knows,' he had said, 'that the animals of the village do not belong to him. So when you catch him eating a goat or a cow he understands he is doing wrong. If you shout at him he will run away.' Perhaps that was all there was to it. If you forget to be afraid, and make enough of a fuss, your enemies invariably turn tail and run.

The next morning I was riding along feeling relatively serene after a good night's sleep, when suddenly I became aware of the sounds of heavy breathing just behind me.

Not ten metres away was a vigorous-looking young Turkana warrior in hot pursuit. He had some sort of head-dress on and was painted up in an outlandish way. In his right hand was a long spear. Instantly, I dug down on the pedals, hunching my shoulders over as much as I could so as to make a smaller target. Still, I expected at any moment to feel the awful thud of his spear. Stones scattered before me. I lurched the bike back from a nasty hole just in time. After a few minutes of not hearing him, I dared take another look. He was nowhere to be seen. I slowed to a stop and tried to make out where he might have gone. The road twisted in and out between and sometimes over the small, barren hills; and I thought he might be to one side, trying to cut me off. Then, as I scanned the path behind me I saw not one but five warriors crest the hill. Five spears reflected the sun. I sped off down the road, praying that it would continue to be ridable. At the top of the next hill, I glanced around. They were about forty metres behind me and coming on fast.

Thankful that the road was more down than up, I hurried on, determined, this time, to put several kilometres between us before stopping again. But all the while I had to dodge rocks, some of which were good-sized boulders, and avoid monstrous pot-holes and skiddy bits of sand. At every odd motion the bike made, I instantly thought: Puncture! Mostly I was sprinting, though every so often I would have to stop and half-carry, half-push my bike across some obstacle. I could not help but look behind me at such times and I was relieved to see that I seemed to be escaping from them. But the road was getting worse. I reached a spot where a small land slide covered it entirely for a hundred metres. I had to walk (stumble – run – lurch) my bike around it, and by the time I got on again the first of the Turkana had reached that spot himself. Were there still four others or had they sent for reinforcements? I sped on, only hoping that the rock pile would give as much trouble to them as it had to me.

Suddenly I saw two figures charging down at me from my right. I dashed on as fast as I dared. For a moment I thought they were going to throw their spears as I whizzed by, but they didn't. They fell in behind me; and once again I was in hearing range of their breathing. 'Oh, God,' I thought. 'Not like this. Please, God. Get me out of here!' I pulled away, fell back again, pulled away, fell back once more. Each time they caught up, the stentorian sounds of their breathing was a little closer. My own chest was splitting. How could they keep this up? But, of course, these were people who ran down their game. When they weren't out collecting heads, these warriors were loping across the desert just for the fun of it.

We had reached the top of a hill and were now starting down the other side. I shifted to a higher gear and suddenly there was nothing to push against. The bloody chain had come off. Instantly, I began to lose speed. Glancing to my right I saw that one of the Turkana was just behind me. This is it, I thought, and prayed that his marksmanship did not equal his running ability. In a minute it would all be over, in any case, for if he did miss, his only slightly slower companion would not. And even if they both missed they would all have another chance when we reached the bottom of the hill. He was up to me now. I tautened for the blow. Then he was running at my side. We were practically rubbing shoulders. What the hell was he doing? Playing cat and mouse? But he wasn't even looking at me. He was looking straight ahead, his face contorted with pain. He was not a young man, and his breath was coming in heavy rasps. Had I been capable of detachment at that moment, I might have observed that he seemed on the point of collapse. Then he passed me, running for all his might down the hill; and as he did he raised his right arm. Now I saw his plan. In a minute he would turn and fling his spear into my chest. 'Oh, my God!' I thought, wondering whether I should risk falling and turn to the side.

And then he threw his spear – at nothing, at a spot in front of him. As it clattered on the ground, he came to a stop. Though he was bent over double, and still breathing like a wounded whale, I glimpsed on his face an undeniable look of satisfaction.

Chapter Thirteen

The North Kenya Desert is a Saturn-scape of black lava rocks, shale and barren hillsides. Apart from the Turkana warriors who sped me on my way, I saw no one for the first three days. Then the vague, constantly disappearing track became a dusty 'road', and thatched huts set up on poles began to appear, in front of which small groups of depressed-looking natives squatted in the dirt. 'Water,' I begged, turning upside down my plastic bottle. Reluctantly, the crone poured me out a litre's worth. 'More,' I demanded, shaking the half-empty container, but her refusal was adamant. Unfriendly, these Turkana, miserly, but none of them, apparently, interested in my head.

I sucked on pebbles – a trick an old Dinka herdsman had taught me – and managed to get to the next meagre source of supply. To my left was sky-blue Lake Turkana the cool sight of which was such a pleasure to the eye – and such a torture to my ever-present thirst; but the wind that blew across it hit me straight in the face, and by mid-afternoon it had usually reached the proportions of a gale. One afternoon, I spent a blissful half hour bathing in its shallows, on the theory that my body would soak up moisture like a sponge; but not only was my thirst all the greater afterwards; my skin was chafed and blistered as well. There were clumps of palms along the shore, and even bands of fishermen; but no one helped me and I could not sit in the shade of a palm tree all day long. With palm fronds I thought to ease my couch at night – until I discovered that it was under them that the vipers loved to lie. Had I been searching for specimens, this knowledge would have been invaluable. As it was, I recoiled in horror when my first viper house de-roofing produced such dramatic results. From that point on I rested my backside safely, if uncomfortably, on bits of jagged rock. Snakes were all around, as populous under the palm fronds – God knows what they did at night – as bathers on a summer's beach. From then on I gave the shores of the lake a miss and camped as far inland as possible. Even so my nights were plagued by nightmares in which, like Tantalus, I would stoop to drink at some cool spring, only to have the water recede. Before my eyes it turned to mud, then clay. Up through a crack would dart a viper's head. The very rushes that had withered away would rise again and strike me with venomous jaws. I cried out, kneeling upright in my tent. Yet I never saw a snake anywhere except under the fronds on the shore of the lake.

Finally I came to the end of the lake and entered a region of such equatorial lushness that it seemed I had died and gone to heaven. Several weary days followed during which I climbed up out of the Valley of Death; and then, right at the top, I strained my left shoulder wrenching my bike back from a pot-hole, and I had to ride into Nairobi with only one hand.

Nairobi was blissful; my friends, the Taylors, most hospitable. They informed me, however, that I might have to stay with them indefinitely as the Tanzanian authorities had closed their border with Kenya and no one, *no one*, was being allowed through. It took a while, but five weeks later I obtained permission. Far be it from them, they finally said, to stop one who had come so far, and been through so much. But I was the only one they let through.

The Africa of my childhood imagination had been populated by the tom-toms of natives and the roar of lions, but so far the nearest I'd come to seeing a dangerous carnivore outside of captivity was when I inadvertently stepped on some leopard droppings while brushing my teeth in the Sudan. Where were the famed herds of wildebeest? In vain I scanned the horizon for the greater, even the lesser, kudu. The sight of Mt. Kilimanjaro, as I approached the Tanzanian border, was magnificent; but where were the zebras? Where were the antelopes, the gazelles? I would have been happy to have seen a few moth-eaten hyenas. Across the Masai Steppe, I rode under a pink cloud of flamingoes; but of the fabled gemsbok I caught but the glimpse of a tail, and of the wild dog only a few stripes.

However, I had no wish to be turned into a nylon-coated hamburger during the night by some sleep-walking elephant; so, when I finished reading the ominous warnings on a park entry sign in Southern Tanzania, I camped where I was. For good measure, I waited until the noonday heat had presumably quieted the local lions before attempting to cross 50 kilometres of what purported to be Africa's best-stocked outdoor zoo.

I was coming to the crest of a hill when from behind it emerged the astonished face of a giraffe – seemingly disembodied. I careered to a stop. It was hardly an awesome beast. What I noticed particularly was the extreme delicacy and beauty of its long eyelashes. It was a bit like looking into the ravaged face of an aged movie queen surprised at her toilette, hair in a twin bun, bandana slightly askew – knot-ends flaring on each side – an expression of startled, though demure, coquettishness. Then the face took on a slight severity: the long, flat nose (or was it lip?) began to wrinkle; and with a disdainful shake, Spotted Beauty turned her head the other way and, rejoined by her body, galloped off.

Next I came upon a rhinoceros browsing in a meadow of wild flowers – at just the right distance from the road. But for his horn, which curved up like a massive carpet tack from between his eyes, he could have been mistaken for a rather bad-tempered-looking cow – a black angus in armadillo skin; a giant pig with a broken-off bit of swill bucket on his head. He certainly did not look dangerous, and I stood there clicking off pictures like any tourist while flowers dribbled from his mouth.

After that I saw and admired a tremendous herd of zebra; the peek-a-boo form of some sort of gazelle; a pair of dik-dik (comely faun-like creatures with enormous, butter-plate eyes). And then, rounding a turn, I suddenly found myself in the midst of a herd of elephants. My instinct was to wheel around and pedal hard the other way, but it was too late for that. Their very aroma seemed to hold me; their invaded silence made all the more ominous by grumblings and foot scrapings and low trumpetings. There was a sense of battle hanging in the air.

Slowly, cautiously, I proceeded to wind my way through the herd. The wrinkled faces, with their baggy eyes and jowl-like ears, suggested the harmless physiognomies of aged aristocrats snoozing off their lunches in the plush security of overstuffed chairs; and I did my best not to disturb them.

But a mother, followed by twin offspring, skittered at the sight of me and went gallumphing off to my left; and I could feel a subtle shift of mood. Directly in front of me a gigantic matriarch blared aloud the news that there was an intruder in their midst. She spread her ears, as if to block my way, pawed the earth with her right forefoot, and waved her trunk back and forth in front of me in just the manner of a wrestler loosening up for a bout.

There was a sturdy-looking tree to my right, but it had no low branches. Behind it loomed the forms of three more elephants, all in good fighting trim. Very slowly, keeping direct eye contact, I circled the beast in front of me, taking care to encroach as little as possible on the territory of others. So far so good, I thought, as I began to round the cape of her backside. Ahead of me, however, the herd swelled on. Sweating profusely, mouth dry as chalk, I cautiously remounted, prepared at an instant to pedal for my life, and continued to run the gauntlet – as slowly, as unobtrusively, as bicycle and terror would permit. I had gone only about fifty metres, when the entire herd began to move.

Now there were currents of elephants; streams that flowed this way and that. I was a rowing boat in the midst of a regatta, a wheelchair patient negotiating the M1 on a bank holiday weekend. I sought and found the protection of another tree and, pressing myself up against its rough bark, closed my eyes. The dust was thick and choking. I prayed that like a boulder in a stream, my tree would remain in place and the current flow around me. The tree shook. Its branches trembled. At any moment I expected it to crash down. I held my breath and tried to detach myself from thoughts of mayhem, while all the elephants in Africa, it seemed, thundered past. And then, abruptly, it was over. Utter stillness. There was not a pachyderm in sight.

Chapter Fourteen

I could see the mist rising from Victoria Falls but because Zambia and Rhodesia (as it then was) were at war, I could not just walk across the bridge. I had to make a detour of 200 kilometres: all the way to Kazungula, where Zambia, Botswana and Rhodesia were delicately joined. Botswana maintained trade with Rhodesia, being dependent on it for food; so one could still cross over there. It was not easy, however. Officials held me up an entire day at both the Zambian and Botswanan borders, and before I actually reached Rhodesia I was forced to camp in a no-man's-land where I was woken in the night by the chatter of automatic weapons and the burst of grenades. The Rhodesians were chasing terrorists back across the border, and I lay there, an unwilling witness to the battle, hoping not to be noticed. My entry into Rhodesia, however, was as smooth as one could wish: the officials polite, efficient and quick. According to the outside world Black Rhodesia was struggling towards independence from repressive colonial rule. Yet the impression I received, immediately, was that the whole country, black as well as white, was fighting against the 'liberators' to retain its existing way of life.

Standing where the great Livingstone had stood, looking down at the Falls, I did not think of any of this. I pulled my cape more tightly around my face and studied the mist-shrouded, mile-long line of water that plunged 355 feet into the boiling gorge below. The continuous roar created a numbness in my ears, and I was suffering from the unaccustomed cold; but I stood there for half an hour or more, watching the play of rainbows in the mist, soaking it all in as it were; until, stiff and shivering, I pushed my bike back into the gloom of the forest and continued on my way to Matetsi.

It was impossible to ignore the political situation, so I kept my eyes on the underbrush; but it was hard to believe that right here, in broad daylight, not more than a month before, a man and his wife had been ambushed. The terrorists struck at random, wherever they could. Any white person was fair game. They had not succeeded with this particular couple, who had instantly jumped out of their armoured car and returned fire, killing one of their assailants and driving off the others. However, there were other, sadder stories; one, of a group of doctors and nurses whose vehicle had been stopped on the very outskirts of Bulawayo. They had been lined up face down on the road; then, one by one, they were shot: three doctors and five nurses – nuns. One of the doctors had lived, had played dead until the terrorists disappeared and the police came. That had happened only two weeks before, and the patrols were everywhere now.

I had been told to restrict my riding to the morning, as the terrorists set up their ambushes in the afternoon so as to be able to escape under cover of darkness. And advised to check in with the police upon arrival. It would be better, of course, if I did not ride at all. I considered ignoring their advice. Perhaps, I thought, if the terrorists saw a cyclist coming towards them, they'd be too surprised to react. On the other hand, 'Who knows – they might take you for a blooming booby-trap.'

Matetsi, Wankie, Dahlia, Lupani; each one a morning's ride. Then there was a jump of a hundred kilometres to Bulawayo. I would spend that night at a hospital compound, the same one that had lost seven of its staff to the terrorists. I was about half way to Matetsi, my mind divided between admiration of the flowering bushes that grew so profusely in this part of Rhodesia, and apprehension about a possible attack, when an armoured truck pulled in front of me, forcing me to stop. Two other vehicles screeched up, and some twenty soldiers piled out and took up defensive positions on both sides of the road. I dropped to the ground and rolled over into a boggy ditch where I folded my arms over my head and instinctively closed my eyes, waiting for the bursts of machine-gun fire.

'Hello, there!' sounded a cheery voice. 'You're the Nor/Africa bloke, right? Sergeant Billie Wilkinson. Just checking you out.' I climbed back on to the road, feeling stupid, and wiped a bit of muck out of my left eye. I asked him, rather stiffly, if he hadn't overdone it a bit. 'Better to be safe than sorry,' he said. 'Bit nasty, this war.' He took me over to the truck. To the left of where the machine-gun was mounted, two dead bodies were sprawled. 'Got these earlier this morning,' he remarked. 'Fourteen yesterday. There're still plenty of them around.'

The Rhodesian army used to hand out photographs of terrorist victims who died under torture, a warning to the Africans who lived on tribal land of what kind of men these 'freedom fighters' were. But the plan backfired. The terrorists used the same photos to scare the villagers into helping them.

'Are you winning, then, do you think?'

'For the moment. But we can't hold out for long.'

There were some white Rhodesians who hated all blacks, who boasted, 'When the time comes, I'll take my share.' These were the ones quoted in the papers. Many I spoke to, however, were resigned to majority rule and hoped it would work, though by then whites were leaving at the rate of a thousand a week.

Those who remained, the doctors and nurses at the hospital compound on that side of Bulawayo, for instance, had developed a fatalistic attitude that I admired them for but also wondered about. The refectory, for example, was open on all sides; and lit up as it was, each of us made a perfect sitting target for any passing marksman. When I asked why they exposed themselves to danger so needlessly, one of them said he would not change his whole way of life just to suit the times, and the others agreed. In a way they seemed almost unconcerned with what might happen to them. Certainly, while I was there, they were much more interested in learning about my trip.

The day before I crossed into South Africa, I spent the night at a farm, the owner of which was an elderly English woman whose husband had been killed years before by a snake. Instead of going back to England, she had stayed on, made a success of it. At first, when I inquired if I could spend the night, she pointed in the direction of the barn. Later we got to talking and she asked me into the house. After I had told her something of my travels, she invited me to dinner; finally, she insisted that I sleep in the guest-room upstairs. She had taken me for a hitch-hiker, she confessed. But to challenge the unknown, as I had, that was something. For what was life without adventure? People had been urging her to return to England. But she had been living in that spot for sixty years. It was her home. Terrorists might kill her, perhaps, but they could not drive her out. And if they tried, they would be in for a few surprises. She might not be able to cycle across the Sahara; but, by Jove, she could dig in and defend a position. And when the time came, *if* it came; the farm workers would side with her. She was quite certain about that.

Chapter Fifteen

The South African immigration officials are notoriously tough on overland travellers. If one doesn't have a certain amount of cash plus an air ticket out of the country, the border is as near Cape Town as one is likely to get. As I had neither, I was surprised and delighted when I was not only admitted but taken round behind the counter for tea and fruit cake.

Unfortunately, the welcome I initially received was not typical of what was to come. The deeper I entered the country the more I found it to be a foreign land. Baobab trees and Boers. No Britons. It was as if they'd won the war with Britain, not lost it. I'd been looking forward to the kind of treatment I'd received in Rhodesia – wined and dined like a hero, for the most part – and here I was either ignored or treated with disdain. Everywhere I felt antagonism, from the hotel clerks who curtly refused me permission to camp in the out-buildings, to the police who locked me up 'for safe-keeping' in their unheated cells. Oddly, what annoyed me most was that virtually no one addressed me in anything but Afrikaans.

It was June, and midwinter in South Africa. The day I rode into Paarl, there was such a storm raging that I was literally blown off my cycle. It was as if a hand had reached down and plucked me off the seat, found me uninteresting, and dropped me again. I booked in at the first hotel, to lick my wounds. Cape Town was only two days away. But between us was a final ridge of mountains. There was no way I could cross the pass in that kind of weather, I was told; but there was also no way I was going to spend another night in that hotel, so near to journey's end. So, the following morning, with the snow flying, I headed for the final obstacle. The snow was ankle-deep in the streets, and it was all I could do to push the bike through.

As I started to climb, however, conditions improved – somewhat. The wind kept the road clear of snow and for short stretches at a time, I was able to ride. It was bitterly cold. My bare legs turned beet-red and the sleet stung my flesh as raw as if it had been buckshot. Yet there was no question of turning back. After coming so far, I could surely make it over one more mountain. And then, mercifully, I became numb; robot-like, almost uncaring.

I crossed the pass, though the mist and snow squalls obscured things to such an extent that the only way I could tell when I had was by the inclination of the road. Going down the other side was even worse. I could not trust myself to let go, even for a moment; for I knew that I would not be able to control myself – that I would hurtle off into oblivion at the next curve. When I reached the bottom, it was dark. All I wanted was shelter and warmth. There was no sign of a hotel, no sign of anything at all at the first crossroad. I was there, almost. But *where* was I? I staggered on for a kilometre or so when at last, out of the sleet, like a mirage, there gleamed the welcoming vision of an inn.

Table Mountain was obscured by thick mist. I couldn't see the tops of the buildings. It was raining: a cold, hard rain. I was consulting a damp street map, trying not to think what I would do if Lloyd's had neglected to transfer my funds, when a bearded bloke came jogging up.

'Can I help you with that?' he said, continuing to jog in place.

'Thank you,' I said. We held the soggy map together.

'Come a long way?'

'Yes, I have. I'm looking for the post office.'

'Let me take you to it. You must be tired from your travels.' And he jogged off.

'Actually, I'm not,' I called out.

'Oh, then you flew in?'

'No, cycled.'

'Jolly good exercise, what? Here for a while?'

'Flying out tomorrow.' He circled back toward me.

'But you bicycled in?'

'Right.'

'Good sport, bicycling. Do a bit of racing myself.'

'I'm a touring cyclist.'

'I see. You go off for a week and camp somewhere, do you?'

'Yes, that's it. Only longer, usually.'

'I say, you wouldn't go off for much longer, not in these parts, would you?'

'Well, I've been in the Transvaal, Rhodesia.'

He stopped and stared at me. 'You don't mean to say you've been cycling in Rhodesia?'

'Actually, I started out in Norway.'

'Let's see, that's near Hopetown, isn't it?'

I saw I'd lost him, but by now we had arrived at the post office. 'I leave you here,' I said.

'Pip, pip, then. Don't run into any tigers.' And he bounded off.

By the next day the weather had cleared. There were sail-boats racing in the harbour. I stood at the Cape of Good Hope and looked down at the swells breaking against the cliffs. Twenty months, it had taken, I could hardly believe it myself.

Chapter Sixteen

Brixham was draped in bunting. A huge banner stretched across the street. Was this for me? Was I finally going to be given a hero's welcome?

'Ian,' someone called. It was one of our neighbours. 'You're home.'

'Yes,' I replied, gesturing vaguely. 'All this . . .'

'Isn't it exciting?'

'What exactly do I do?'

'Oh, it's not too late.'

'Should I go back and come in again?'

'Pity you weren't here, though.'

'What?'

'Yesterday. The big day.'

'You mean I've missed it?'

'You can still celebrate.'

'Celebrate what?' The words hung there in the air.

'Why, the Queen's Silver Jubilee of course. My, you have been gone a long time, haven't you?'

I got away from her as quickly as I could and rode down to the quay. It was a favourite place of mine. I stood there for a while, looking out at the boats, trying to put my mind at rest. How flat it all seemed, suddenly. For the next few days the phone would be ringing and Dad would be shouting out for someone to answer it. Mum would be terribly excited and we'd talk too much. *The Herald Express* and *The Western Morning News* would be sending reporters round. I would have to get my slides together for the series of talks I was giving in America.

I'd forgo the hero's welcome and go home for a cup of tea.

I laughed. I'd been upstaged all my life, come to think of it. On the South American/Alaska trek I'd been beaten out of a spot on Johnny Carson's television show by a 400-pound turtle, the Darien Gap adventure had been overshadowed by the survival of a family after their boat had been lost because of killer whales – at the moment of victory there was always something else. This time it was the Queen.

Part 3

The Peruvian Gap

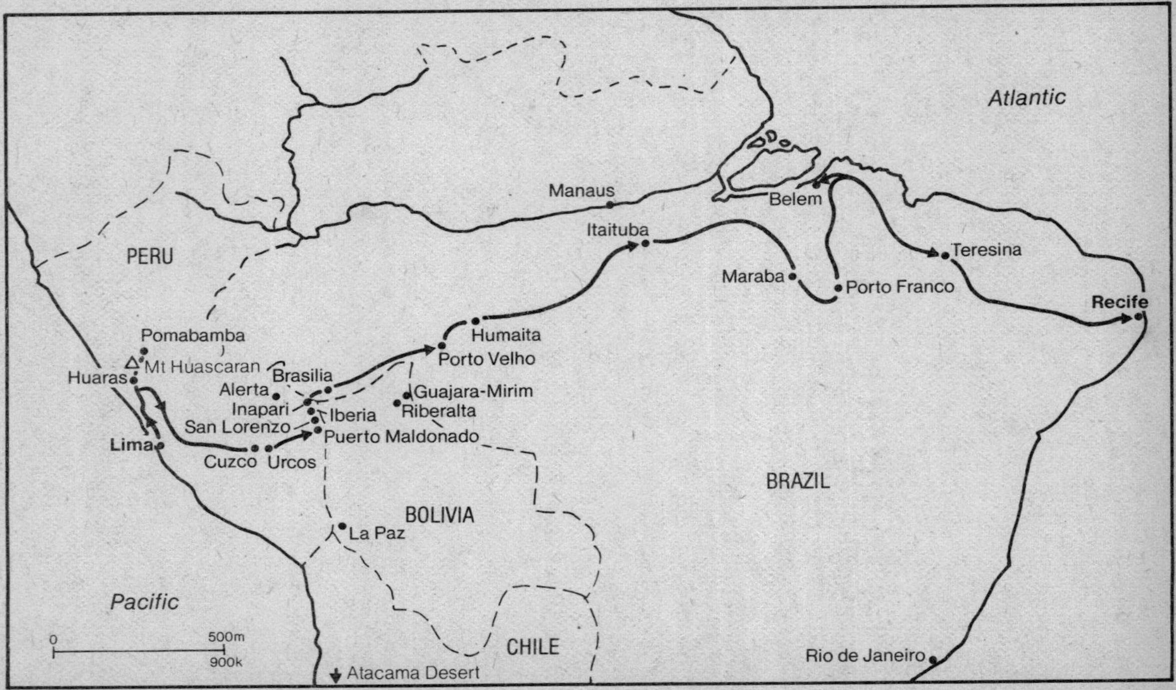
Atlantic
Manaus
Belem
Itaituba
Teresina
Maraba
Porto Franco
Recife
PERU
Pomabamba
Mt Huascaran
Huaras
Humaita
Porto Velho
Brasilia
Alerta
Guajara-Mirim
Inapari
Iberia
Riberalta
San Lorenzo
Puerto Maldonado
Lima
Cuzco
Urcos
BRAZIL
BOLIVIA
La Paz
Pacific
0
500m
900k
CHILE
Atacama Desert
Rio de Janeiro

Chapter One

I met Jean at a lecture I gave in Ashbury just a year after I returned to England from my Nor/Africa trip. It wasn't much of a lecture, really. The fellow who'd arranged it had put us in the back room of a pub. There were about thirty people squeezed in, most of them sitting on the floor; and Peter, my assistant, was very anxious to get it over with so we could get home that night. It was the last show of a two-week tour, and he ran through the slides so fast I could barely get out where we were before he was off to the next. I noticed Jean right away. She sat in front, just beneath me; legs crossed, dark ringlets framing her face. I couldn't take my eyes off her.

Afterwards, when we moved into the main bar for a drink, she handed me a beer. 'Could you please give me some advice,' she said. 'I'm thinking of going to Turkey, and I don't know anything about it. Do you suppose I'll be all right alone?' She was very beautiful. Her eyes were hazel, and even in the dim light they shone with what seemed to me an uncommon intensity.

'Turkey,' I said. 'That's a dangerous place for a young girl.'

'Oh, I've been to Ireland,' she said.

I had to smile. She was so eager, so naïve. Three weeks later I happened to be back in Ashbury. I'd just set up my bike for a two-week display in a shop window, when in came Jean. She was with two young men.

'Ah,' she said, walking right over to me, not registering the least surprise. 'You short-changed me, you know. I'm the one who bought you that beer.'

'Yes, of course,' I said smiling. 'Do you still want to visit Turkey?'

What if she disguised herself as a boy? she asked. Wouldn't that make it less dangerous? We talked for a while about the problems. 'Why Turkey anyway?' I said, finally. 'If you're set on going, why not pick some really exotic place? Japan, for instance. Or Indonesia.' She didn't respond, seemed to be thinking about that. 'Everyone goes to Turkey,' I added, more to fill the silence than anything else. 'Actually, I'm going to South America in a month's time. Why don't you come with me?'

I expected . . . I don't know what I expected. For her to laugh? Anything. Except what actually happened.

'Would you take me?' she said.

I didn't answer her directly. Instead, I babbled on about how difficult it all was: how tired you got of camping, of being dirty, of eating the same food day in and day out; how boring it became, the biking; how you grew to hate it. A week's trip was great fun, if the weather was good, if you didn't have any bad luck, and if you managed to stay on speaking terms with your companions. But touring for month after month was no sort of life. The very things you went for, either they didn't happen, they weren't there, or they turned into horrors. No, it was much better to stay at home and read about it, I said. I was laying it on a bit thick, admittedly. But I wanted to see how she'd react.

'But you love it,' she said, when I finished. 'Why?'

'Oh, there're compensations.' I shrugged my shoulders.

'Tell me about *them*.'

To tell the truth, I was playing with her. I had the rest of the afternoon to kill before my train came; so, for the moment, I allowed my fantasies free rein. I saw the way her hair licked up from her forehead in little wisps and found myself imagining her face framed in sleep.

'Jean can do it all right, if that's what you're worried about,' said Doug. 'She's a sticker.'

'It's a great opportunity for her, I'd say,' added Colin. They actually seemed to be pushing her off on to me. Why?

'I leave in a month. You couldn't be ready that soon.'

'I think I could.'

It was getting near time for my train. I'd have to hurry. 'Go home and think about it,' I said. 'In a week's time, if you're still keen, give me a call.'

We ran into the station, the four of us. There was the train, on the point of departure. I threw my bag up and jumped in just in time.

'Ian!' Jean shouted. 'Where do I contact you?' I was about to give her my brother's phone number – I was off to his place for a week's visit – when I checked myself.

'If you're that interested,' I called out, 'you'll find me.' She looked puzzled and shouted something, but the train had started and I couldn't hear. I leaned out of the window until she was out of sight. All the way to Maurice's house I thought, what had I done? Why hadn't I sewn it up? 'You're a fool, Hibell,' I told myself. 'You'll never see that girl again.'

Four days later she telephoned me. Did I still want to take her? She had had half her jabs already. The money was all arranged. 'There's one thing,' said Jean. 'You don't have to. I made them promise. But my parents would like to meet you.'

'I should think so,' I said, and laughed, but she didn't join in.

'No, really, Ian, you needn't if you don't want to.'

'But I do,' I said. 'In the meantime, could you come down to Brixham?'

I met her at the station two days later. She was smaller than I remembered; and quite pale: ill, from the injections. Mum took an immediate liking to her, and vice versa. She warmed her way into Dad's heart, too, with a goodnight kiss. 'Here, love. You take up the tray,' I heard Mum say to her next morning. She stayed and chatted with Dad while he ate his breakfast. I hadn't heard him sound so happy in years.

We made lists. We got things together. I started work on her bike. And a week later we visited her parents. Her father left for his room immediately after dinner, as he had to be up early the next morning to fly to Brussels on business. He was a tall, bespectacled man; interested, but a bit detached.

'You should have seen Daddy when I told him,' Jean said. Her mother smiled. '"Remember that cyclist I met? The one who rode across the Sahara and was rescued by the Tuaregs and all that?" "Yes." "He's asked me to go with him to Peru." He made the most awful choking sound. I suppose I should have waited till he finished his soup.'

Mrs Beasley, on the contrary, had liked the idea from the first. An older, experienced man to protect her daughter. Much better than her going off to Turkey by herself. 'And you two do seem to get on.' I felt myself begin to redden. 'You'll be using the same tent, I suppose,' she added, with just a touch of archness in her voice.

'Ian's already said how important it is to keep the weight down.' Dear Jean. She had already sawn the end off her plastic hairbrush.

Jean had lived more in her 23 years than I had in my 44, I soon found out. She was very open about it. She'd been in love with Doug, had shared a flat with him for a while; but Doug had become involved with another girl named Claire, now Jean's best friend; in fact, they had had a baby. Claire and Doug weren't living with each other at the moment, however; Doug and Colin (the other boy she'd been with at our second meeting) were sharing a flat right now. There were others, I gathered, who wandered in and out.

Jean had opted out of university to live with a boy named Simon when she was seventeen. For two years they'd managed a little farm. She had also been a chef in a local restaurant. The head chef had taught her French cuisine; and, in a few months, the restaurant had built up such a name for itself that they were turning people away. Most recently she had worked in 'the largest private nursery in England', where she had specialized in pyracanthas.

'Isn't it crowded, all jammed together like that?' I'd asked her, thinking of how much I would dislike her living arrangements.

'Not really,' she said. 'I take care of the baby when Claire's painting. Sometimes we go for walks. Doug picks up occasional work. We talk.'

'Don't you ever feel like getting a place of your own?'

'Sometimes. I suppose everyone does.' Doug and Claire and Colin and the others, they were her real family, I discovered. They gave her the security she needed. And the freedom. She wouldn't be doing this, she said, without them.

Chapter Two

I pushed out hard, shielded by the Renault, pedalling fiercely to keep inside its tail. The traffic whooshed by just behind me, and I coasted to a stop and looked back to see where Jean was. Through the stream of cars, I could glimpse her poised there, waiting for another vehicle to plunge out into the oncoming rush so she could use it, as I had, to get across. Lima traffic was bad enough at two in the afternoon, but now, with everyone trying to get home at once, the cold, grey winter's dusk making it hard to see, it was particularly dangerous to be riding. I cursed the absence of traffic lights, and watched a VW Beetle whip out toward me. Jean was still there, hoping for a better chance.

For Jean, particularly, it had been a hard day: tired to begin with from the all-night flight from Los Angeles, held in customs for hours while I rebuilt the bikes, depressed by the ride in from the airport – past the ugly cardboard-and-tin shanty towns; reaching the embassy only to find that Señor Ramon and his wife lived fifteen kilometres out of town and back the other way; it was hardly the perfect introduction to bicycle touring in a foreign country. Jean was game. She was more than adequately prepared. But this was all new to her, and I felt her very much in my charge. I pulled out the map to check the route once again. We were almost there: one kilometre on this road, a bit of a jog around where they were building some blocks of flats, two more kilometres, and we would be at the new home of my friend Enrique Ramon, wealthy farmer turned industrialist.

I looked up to see a pale-faced Jean coast by. 'You all right?' I called out. She nodded and I pushed off, taking up the lead again. In another half-hour it would be dark. Enrique had told me over the phone that his mid-life change of career was involuntary and had been made 'to accommodate the wishes of my government'. He had laughed, somewhat grimly, and added, 'But wait till you see the new house. And swim in the pool.' When Steve and David and I had unknowingly trespassed on his lawn, he had welcomed us in for breakfast with exuberance. 'You don't look like *banditos* to me,' he had said, after coming down himself to investigate. We had spent three days as his guests: lazing on his patio, wandering through his vineyards; listening to his political views, hearing about his country's problems. They had left him the house of his parents and 15 acres. But he had to be closer to his factory – where he made boxes. 'Wooden crates and boxes. Believe me, it does not take genius.'

We were in a much better area now. Behind high walls

and thick hedges one could glimpse white stucco, iron railings, red roof tiles, even the occasional glimmer of a pool. 'Pot-hole,' I called out, pointing with my left hand, feeling Jean swerve with me. Only a few minutes more, I told myself, already beginning to relax.

Número Siete. There were three large cars parked in front of the house. I gave Jean's hand a squeeze while we waited for the servant to bring 'mine host'. The door opened again. 'Ian. How nice to see you,' said Señora Ramon. 'But you didn't tell us you were married?'

'This is Jean Beasley, my travelling companion,' I said, with studied emphasis. Jean extended her hand.

'I'm sorry,' Señora Ramon said, stepping back abruptly, 'Enrique should have told you. The house is full.' I didn't know what to say. It was so transparently obvious that she was giving us the brush-off. She wasn't looking at Jean, or at me, but at the cars. 'We have people staying with us, relatives of Enrique's. Every room is occupied.'

'I understand,' I said, my own voice frostily polite. 'Please tell Enrique how sorry we were to miss him.'

'If there's anything we can do,' she said, hardly able to make her voice sound civil.

I motioned to Jean. We had no time to lose. Where we would find a place to camp I had no idea; but the task would be considerably more difficult after dark. The only place I could think of was the construction site we had passed. I did not feel like testing the benevolence of the neighbours, and as for riding back into Lima to look for a hotel, it would be difficult enough to go two kilometres without lights. 'Ruddy bitch!' I said, as we pulled out of the drive. 'We'll have to camp.' Jean made no response. 'There's a good place a bit further back.' She simply followed me in silence.

It was hardly the ideal camping spot – trenches everywhere, piles of earth. And I knew that we might be chased off in the middle of the night. I didn't dare set up the tent. That would be like waving a flag. If we got out at first light, we'd be all right, I thought. I tried to explain to Jean that these Peruvian women were back in the Middle Ages as far as non-married relationships were concerned, but she was huddled up in her sleeping bag by this time and I could get no response from her. As for myself, I could not sleep. How stupid, I kept thinking. Here it was, our first night, and already I had let her down. We could have stayed in Lima. The next day would have been soon enough to visit the Ramons. How could I have so forgotten the prejudices of these people? Yet in my letter I had said that there was a young woman accompanying me. Surely Enrique could have warned me off if that was going to be an embarrassment to his wife. Could he possibly not have told her? Did he tell her, and did she make a scene? Insist on her way? Was that why she had come to the door and not he? And I had thought him such a man; so much my friend. Jean was asleep. In the dim light her face appeared calm, almost serene. She had eaten nothing, had said hardly a word. I hoped that by morning she would be herself again.

It was light in the east when I awoke with a start to see a shawled figure hovering over me. '*Peligroso!*' the lips whispered. She was the archetypal crone, the proverbial witch. My impulse was to cross myself. Had I had a weapon I would certainly have brandished it.

'*Qué pasa?*' I finally stuttered out.

'*Banditos*,' she hissed, making throat-slitting motions with her hands.

Who was this woman? How had she found us? Should I reach out and grab her? But already she was gone. I knew that it was never prudent to camp in or around any city. The countryside was relatively safe, but where the cardboard-and-tin villages of the desperate existed there was danger. Yet I had had to camp near such places sometimes, and nothing had ever happened to me; and we were ten kilometres from the airport and its slums. Even if we heeded your warning, crone, where would we go? But what about her? Hadn't she perhaps been caught in the act of stealing? I placed the valuables bag closer to my head and put my arm through its strap. But I did not think it was likely she would come back.

'Ian!' The sun was shining brightly. There was the sound of a truck grinding along in low gear very close by. Men's voices. I blinked my eyes. 'Your bag: it's gone!' Jean was frantically rummaging through our things. 'The tent. The water bottles. Your clothes bag!' The strap to the valuables bag had slipped off my arm in the night, but everything was there: our passports, the camera, our money. Fortunately, I'd gone to bed with my clothes on. Otherwise I'd have had to ride to Lima in the nude, I told Jean. She was not amused. Had the crone come back? I wondered. Or were we indeed lucky that our lives had not been taken as well? In all my travels nothing had ever been stolen from me before. But then, I thought, up until last night no friend had ever refused me hospitality, either.

'We'll have to ride back to Lima and see about another tent,' I said, packing up as quickly as I could. Hoping to look both innocent and inconspicuous, we walked our cycles to the road. No one questioned us.

An hour later, in a government office in the centre of Lima, we were talking with the Sports Minister, Señor Arnoa. 'You will take my tent,' he insisted. It would be several weeks before a new one arrived from the States, and in the meantime we could ride to Huarez. 'Before you embark on such a hazardous venture, you should see something of Peru,' he said. Huarez was situated in the Huascaran National Park – one of the most beautiful areas in the world, he assured us. There were twenty-seven peaks over 17,000 feet. He himself had made two first ascents. Not to go there was like travelling to Nepal without visiting Mount Everest. He would arrange everything for us. All we needed to do was buy me some clothes.

When we returned, we could discuss our route across the Andes. 'This is a paradise I send you to. Believe me.' Jean was smiling, happily. When we left his office, however, her face took on a worried expression. 'We're not going to camp out tonight, are we Ian?'

'No, we'll find a hotel.'

'And a nice restaurant?'

'I suppose then you'll want to go dancing.'

Jean laughed and tugged me by the arm. 'Come on,' she said, mischievously, 'you know you can't dance. I want to get to our room.'

Chapter Three

Jean was leading. The morning overcast had cleared and the desert stood out in stark relief. Already the heat waves were beginning to rise. Not that it was all that hot in September – nothing like the sizzling pan Steve and David and I had ridden across five years before. Still, it was not something the ordinary person would enjoy. Yet here was Jean, positively exuberant. The Atacama Desert agreed with her, she said. She loved the heat. It was I who stopped first. 'You should have brought that Arab headgear of yours,' she said to me, teasing, as I sat there mopping my brow. And then she wheeled around, her eyes bright with amusement, and flew off again – as carelessly, as lightly, as a butterfly.

Half an hour later, she was talking to a little girl who was standing in front of a lean-to made of pieces of tin and rotting cardboard. 'The poor thing,' said Jean. 'Look at where she lives.' The child, who was four or five years old, was holding a corner of her filthy dress up to her mouth in one grubby, tight-fisted hand. So absorbed was Jean in the child that she did not see the black-cloaked woman emerge from another building and come striding over.

She grabbed the child, indignantly, then stood there like a statue, waiting for us to leave. I thought for a moment that Jean might do something impetuous. She was capable of it, certainly. I'd seen her, with some admiration, give as good as she got to a group of field workers who shouted at her from the back of a truck the day before. But she mounted her cycle and sped off without a word.

We had turned inland by then and were climbing up a broad valley. It was just as hot as before, hotter perhaps, and we were riding into a wind – up through an *arroyo* that was perhaps a mile wide, tilted sharply upwards but otherwise as flat as a parking lot, except where boulders dotted the surface, a reminder that in the rainy season this central gorge was a boiling flood.

'What did she suppose I was going to do?' complained Jean during one of our breaks. She was still seething.

As we got into the mountains, however, the people became more friendly. The scenery began to live up to the promises I had made, too; and Jean started to enjoy herself – in just the way I'd hoped. It was hard going, but she never complained. And then we hit the gravel.

We'd ridden on dirt roads in California, but this was different: wash-outs, containing rocks the size of your hand, stretching half-way across the road. It wasn't so bad climbing, but when you hit a loose bit at a curve barrelling along at 20 m.p.h. you had to know how to skid. Though she didn't want to admit it, Jean was scared.

'Relax,' I told her. She threw me a scathing look and tried again. She was braking too much, as usual. Wouldn't let herself go. When she came to the curve she was rigid; though the road stretched before her in a graceful arc, she wobbled around it as if on a tightrope.

Our two weeks had extended to a month, and we were committed, now, to touring the whole range. Yet we weren't getting anywhere. Around every corner, it seemed, I would find her sitting by the side of the road, staring off into the distance. 'I'm looking at the view,' she said. 'Isn't that why we came?' What was the point of being surrounded by so much beauty, if you were too busy watching the road to enjoy it? I explained that you couldn't brake all the time and expect to get anywhere. You had to take a few chances, maybe some spills. You had to go with a touch of abandon – sweep round the curves as if you were cutting letters on the ice.

'You want me to hurt myself? Is that what you're saying?'

'Of course not.'

'You do. All you care about is the daily mileage.'

Usually, when we stopped to camp, there was a routine we went through that made this, in many ways, the best time of the day. We'd find a spot that looked out over the valley, or up at a mountain, not too near any huts or villages: a flat place, where there was water. The trick, too, was to stop early enough so that the tent was pitched, and the food ready well before darkness came. Ideally, we would be cleaning up the last of whatever Jean had prepared, smacking our lips, sucking our fingers, pouring coffee, as the sky blazed purple. For when darkness fell, it immediately became cold. Quickly, we would crawl into our tent and snuggle into our sleeping bags. And then, if all had gone well, came the best time of all. For Jean was normally as loving and affectionate as she was strong and determined. All cosy in our little world, we would chatter away about our lives, the day, the days to come, anything at all; and all the while our bodies would become warmer, our hearts more aroused; until, invariably, we would melt, deliciously, into one another's arms.

Now, however, the end of the day was a miserable affair. Afraid to speak for fear of stirring up some bitterness, I would all too often eat in virtual silence. At first Jean tried to brave it out, pretending that there was nothing wrong; but she couldn't hide her feelings. Awake in the night, I would hear her crying softly, huddled away from me in the tent. Often she would blow her nose, or sigh, or say she felt a cold coming on: try to disguise what it was in some way; but I could always tell at a glance how she was feeling, and I knew she was miserable. Finally, one evening, it came to a head.

'You want me to go home. Don't lie to me. I know you do.'

'I do not. It's the last thing I want. I . . . '

'You hate me. You wish I'd never come.' She was crying now, sobbing uncontrollably. I tried to put my arm around her but she shook it off. Pulling on my jacket I crawled out of the tent and walked off toward the edge of the slope, hoping she would cry herself out. Had I pushed her too hard? Perhaps we should never have come. We could have stayed at Ragged Point, where it all began . . .

'Ian. Don't ask questions. Just walk down that path.' I'd just finished setting up the tent, but Jean was packing up again. 'I'll make some tea,' she added. Wondering what was up, I went off.

Beneath me was a crescent of white sand, obstructed only by a few small islands of rock, that stretched to a point about a mile away. No people. No houses. It was hard to believe that such a place existed so near to Santa Barbara. It took us almost an hour to transport all our things down to the beach, but once we were there we felt as if this was our own desert island. We set the tent up again in a grassy spot back from the beach, and spent the late afternoon exploring our kingdom. The thunderous waves made swimming impossible, and the water was too cold, in any case; but we dashed in and out of the surf like children, made a huge bonfire, and when darkness came we could look out past the combers at the lights of the fishing boats and imagine that this was our home, that we had lived here for years.

It was our first real camping. After two weeks on a bus, heaven indeed. That very evening I lost all my shyness; and what had been occupying my mind for weeks as a seemingly insoluble problem, was sweetly and lovingly resolved. It was like a miracle, for I had almost lost hope she would ever think of me in that way. On the bus she had usually rejected the proffered arm, preferring to curl up with her head anywhere but on me. Yet she was hardly prudish, and certainly not shy. I thought of the day we left Brixham for her parents' house. She was about to strap up her pack, when she opened it instead and took off her shirt. Just like that, without turning around or anything. She caught me looking at her, and laughed. 'Come, come, Ian. We'll be seeing a lot more of each other than this, I suppose.' And then she pulled a shirt out of her pack and put it on.

I had fallen in love with Jean practically at first sight. But I never imagined she would reciprocate my feelings. It seemed I had always worshipped women from afar; yet here we were, as natural and loving a pair as anyone could wish. In the months that followed, during our long loop up the coast through Yosemite, Jean had her moments of doubt. She said she felt plagued, sometimes, with feelings of guilt. There were unresolved aspects of her life that I could never fully know about. Yet all the while our relationship grew deeper, more secure. If I was considerably older than she was, our obliviousness to that fact was to me one of the attendant wonders. By the time we left for Peru and the start of our transcontinental tour, we were not only well-prepared physically; in my mind we were as good as married . . .

Jean had joined me at the edge of the slope. She had her arm around my waist, her face snuggled up against my shoulder. We held each other for a long time. What did it matter, I thought, if we spent the rest of our lives in these mountains. What did anything matter except us. 'I'll learn,' she whispered. 'Please. Just let me.' I hugged her to me more closely, afraid to speak. 'Oh, Ian,' she murmured, tears in her voice. 'My love. My love.'

Chapter Four

As we climbed the road up to Mt. Huascaran, I couldn't help worrying about how Jean was going to manage the descent. This was the steepest road yet, with the tightest curves. All day we climbed: up and up; until, near evening, we reached the famous Lakes of Langui y Layo that we had come so far to see. Hidden there in a lush, marshy valley, the twin bodies of water perfectly reflected the glacier and the peaks of Mt. Huascaran that towered, glittering, behind them. It was the picture of serenity: no breath of wind; the pale green water smooth as ice – a magical setting. And then came the flies, and a mad rush to set up the tent. Poor Jean. She was specially vulnerable to insect bites. Before she could crawl to safety, she was one gigantic welt.

As soon as we stepped outside the tent the next morning, they fell upon us, each bite drawing cries of pain. 'Let's *go!*' yelled Jean, and she flew through the packing-up procedure in record time; was on her bike and off down the road before I'd taken down the tent.

'Hold on!' I cried, but I could not catch her. I saw her once, far below me, perched like a jockey, careening around a switchback.

When I reached the valley some hours later, after a descent that would have brought a cold sweat to the brow of Evel Knievel, there she was sitting on a rock, grinning her silly head off. 'Thought you'd taken the short way down,' I said, coming to a stop.

'That was fun!' she beamed. 'I *couldn't* stop; they'd have eaten me alive.'

The spell was broken. From that point on there was no holding Jean back. One day we covered 50 kilometres; in mountains like these, something of a record. And because we went so fast in between times, we could afford to dally. Each village we came to was unique; each mountain pass; each valley. Sometimes there was the thrill of danger shared: the afternoon we outraced a thunderstorm and stood trembling beneath an overhang as the lightning crackled and the rain poured down. Other times we came upon sights so awesome they will be forever branded on our minds: waterfalls that seemed to disappear into the tree-tops, clouds billowing over snow-blinding peaks, precipices that would make an eagle dizzy. Jean's first llama! The herd of llamas that blocked the road, the grumpy shepherdess with the bowler hat and pipe. Jean's laugh echoing through a valley.

One village was perched on the side of a hill, the houses literally built on top of each other: a 30-storey apartment building where everyone knew everyone else intimately and even the old had a bounce to their walk as they climbed the stairs. There was another village that slept in the hollow of a valley; so peaceful, so protected: fields of maize trim as garden plots; a sanctuary filled with birds and the sounds of water and children. Fifty pairs of hands reached out to touch us as we rode by. A little boy threw his arms around Jean's waist and would not let her go. Our bicycles were taken from us and the competition to see who would push them was severe. It was as if we were favourite aunts and uncles come from afar; yet this was just the customary way these isolated people greeted strangers.

We would stay for a day, three days, even longer, when a particular place caught our fancy; and always Jean would talk to the women, the children, everyone. She had a talent for communicating with people that I certainly did not possess and that I had never witnessed in anyone else to such a degree. Checking over our cycles, I would overhear her giving advice to the women in her imperfect but musical Spanish – about everything from how to prepare *coq au vin* to methods of birth control. 'Do you really think you should be talking about such things to these people?' I asked her one day. 'They do have their own ways, you know.'

'And some of them have more children than they want, too,' Jean said.

There was only one problem. Everywhere we went Jean was besieged by admirers. Not only did young men gaze after her with sheep's eyes, but they slipped her notes. 'What does that one say?' I demanded one morning.

'That I should escape from my papa and meet my lover down by the stream.'

'Your papa? Is that what you told them?'

'It's what they thought, silly.'

In some places I was her uncle, in others her brother. In most, admittedly, I was her husband, but Jean loved to tease and she knew that nothing got to me quite like being called, 'father'. It wasn't just boys, either, who were attracted to her, but men in general. In a way, of course, I rather liked it. It was flattering. Yet it was also tiresome, having to be constantly on guard. I couldn't leave Jean's side if we were in a café, for instance, without there being several *caballeros* in attendance when I returned.

It all came to a head in the village of Pomabamba. We'd been there for ten days, longer than we'd stayed anywhere else, and everyone knew us – and adored Jean. Particularly admiring was the local school-teacher, Roberto. When I saw him in the café seated at a table, I groaned inwardly. Swaying dangerously, for he was quite drunk, he gestured us over. With a sweep of his arm he offered Jean a seat. For the sake of Anglo-Peruvian relations! The first round of drinks was on him. Several beers later, a group of dancers passed the door. Ah ha, he said, reeling towards them. You must dance for us. An extra rehearsal for the fiesta. A command performance – for the *Inglésa* – for the *Inglésa* queen. And he made Jean go outside and receive the bows. Far from resenting his behaviour, the group seemed delighted. Right there in the street, the musicians took up their places and the dancers divided into two columns: one representing the conquistadors, haughty and proud; the other the Incas, subservient and fearful. The harp sounded and the fiddle screeched and *El baile de los huancas* began. They had no costumes, only their swords; but it was not difficult to distinguish between their roles or imagine the bloody slaughter their actions mimed. Jean took it all in as if she were a child attending her first circus.

When the performance was over, the troupe crowded into the café. The leader bowed to Jean and held out his hand. 'He wants you to dance!' exclaimed a rapturous Roberto.

'But I don't know how,' she protested, rather too gaily.

'They will show you,' he announced, and sweeping her up, gave her hand to the dancer. The musicians struck up a lively gig, the crowd cheered; and, giving me a mischievous look, Jean kicked off her sandals and allowed herself to be led into the middle of the circle of men. A handkerchief was produced and given to her – a talisman. Soon she was dancing with enthusiasm; then with abandon. Her bare arms glistened; moisture stood out on her brow. The café became packed with men. Brown faces leered, feet began to stamp. I could no longer see her for the press of the crowd.

When the music finally stopped, there were cheers, shouts of *gringita*. The men who had not been able to get into the café, joined in. When at last Jean was returned to me, I felt like one of the Roman guards assigned to protect the vestal virgins in the Forum. She was exhausted and wanted to sit down, but I decided it was time to go home. There was entirely too much ogling going on for my comfort.

Out in the street she peered around. 'Where are all the women? Never any women. Only men allowed to roam the streets.' She was right, of course. It was one of the things the young women had complained to Jean about. The men spent the evenings in the cafés, but the women had to stay at home and mind the children. Even when there were no children. What could I say? She glared a bit, then gave a rather short laugh, and we continued on our way.

Roberto had offered to escort us to the fiesta in the morning. 'He'll not remember his promise,' I said. But I was wrong. He came bright and early. For more than an hour we climbed a twisting, mountain path. Others had started before us, for the fiesta was in full swing when we arrived. From our perch we could see the line of revellers winding up the steep pasture from the river-side shrine far below. Huge effigies, painted in gold and red, balanced precariously on the shoulders of stoical-looking Indians, their eyes glazed from too much *chicha*, their progress faltering, each stumble greeted by hoots of laughter. Surrounding each effigy, however, as if to protect it, was a large crowd of Sunday-best-dressed men and women: a field of brightly-coloured shawls and ponchos, dotted with new black bowler hats. Suddenly a rocket burst above the procession; there were great billows of smoke, the whooshing sounds of more rockets; scattered explosions above and around the revellers. A hideous cacophony struck our ears. A series of tangled chords, perhaps three to four bars in length, were repeated, endlessly, as the stupefied musicians, their tall, V-shaped instruments held high, stumbled uphill after the tottering effigies. Charred sticks fell into the crowd and instantly there was a scuffle among the small boys to recover them. Violins screeched, and shepherd's pipes sent piercing screams out over the valley. The effigies passed us and made their way into the church. Behind them came the *huanquillas*, masked dancers whose costumes suggested the armoured uniforms of the Spanish conquerors. It was a repetition of the dance we had seen the previous evening. When those portraying the Incas threw off their bonds and pranced exultantly, heads held high, we did not have to be told that they had just won freedom from their oppressors.

Attention shifted to the church where the giant effigies were lined up against the wall. When they were all in place, a high-pitched, nasal voice began to intone the mass – at breakneck speed. This lasted for perhaps three minutes. When it was over there was a joyous burst of music, real music; and the crowd began to shout and move about. The formal part of the fiesta was over. Participants and observers mixed, beer and *chicha* flowed. A group of 'soldiers' approached. One by one they came up to Jean, bowed low, and doffed their high peaked hats. Had it not been that their moustached masks – surrealistically oversized, cheeks painted a bright pink, the bluest of eyes – were too securely affixed, no doubt each would have followed this display with a beery kiss.

They turned out to be the dancers of the night before. Their leader saluted. 'They want me to dance again,' said Jean. '*Gringita!*' a voice shouted from the crowd. It was Manuel, the scoundrel I'd caught two days before slipping a note under our door. 'We'd better go,' she said, pressing herself closer to my side. But the crowd hemmed us in. Suddenly, above the general bedlam, I heard the sound of angry voices. A fist struck out. Another. And then the contestants were rolling on the ground and I could see no more. A stout man in a filthy shirt, little pig eyes blazing, roughly pushed me aside. Another man grabbed him and now the two were struggling, staggering, falling. Bleary faces were staring at us from all sides. Manuel was pushing toward us. I looked around for help. Where was Roberto? The leader of the dancers was not far off, but he was propped up between two fellow 'soldiers', a bottle of *chicha* raised to his lips. 'Ian! Help!' A man had pushed in between us. I shouted something and grabbed him by the shoulder, forced my way in front of Jean: head buried, elbows flailing, like a scrum-half fighting for the ball. How long I battled my way forward I have no idea, but finally I broke free of the surging, drunken mass of humanity. Jean grabbed my hand, and we ran across a field littered with bottles and papers and sprawled-out bodies; past the deserted church, and toward the path that wound down the mountain to Pomabamba.

'I told you you'd gone too far,' I said, back in our room.

'What do you mean?' she replied, angrily.

'You know perfectly well you invite these things.' Giving me a look that would have withered a peach, Jean began stuffing clothes into her bag.

That night we stayed in a grass hut among the acacias and giant cacti of a mini-desert between two mountain ranges. The cacti had just bloomed and their small, white bells were everywhere; asparagus-like stalks, some of them fifty feet high, stood out like grim sentinels against the sky. In the next village there was also a fiesta in progress, but here troupes of young girls walked sedately through the streets, holding bouquets of flowers. Their arms were covered in bracelets and ribbons; their elaborately-made costumes were inlaid with beads and tiny mirrors. And by their sides young men in white shirts and black pants carried on their shoulders statues of the Virgin.

Chapter Five

I am not what you might call highly experienced when it comes to women. Women puzzle me, in fact, always have. Take Jean. Jean adores children, all children, particularly little Peruvian boys. Yet here she was acting like Queen Boadicea – I could practically see the knives twirling in her wheels – and the gaggle of boys she was riding down with such blood-curdling yells were leaping for their lives off the side of the road. Why was she so furious? Because, egged on by their elders, they had been casting a few well-aimed stones in our direction. In Chavin, which we were approaching, there was an Inca fort, a virtually mandatory stop for every foreign visitor to the country. The result? A general detestation of foreigners. All quite natural and to be expected. We'd even discussed it. What one did was put one's head down and make tracks. What one did not do was dismount and show annoyance. Decidedly one did not hurl handfuls of gravel and call out names. We were lucky their aim wasn't still better. A bruised calf and a few lumps on the back were practically badges of honour. None of this, however, Jean's view. 'The little bastards!' she kept saying. There was no calming her down.

And then, in the middle of the night, someone threw a rock at our tent that ripped through the fly-sheet and made a good dent in the ground. To Jean this sort of behaviour was incomprehensible, and it cancelled out brighter moments: the song a shepherd played her the day before on his flute, the crowd of children in that isolated village, vying with each other for the honour of pushing her bicycle. I had lain awake half the night waiting for more rocks to fall, greeted the morning with gratitude when we were safe. But Jean was still grinding her teeth.

And then she was so upset when we reached our first mail pickup and there were no letters for her. You get to expect that, I told her. If you ever receive your mail in places like this, you take it as some kind of miracle. Her letters were probably gathering soup stains on the desk of some minor official, or being ground into the floor of a *bodega*; or, possibly, flying in the wind, traversing the country all on their own: whirling in shreds through the mountain passes.

'Very amusing. And what news from dear old Mum?'

'Things pretty much the same. Dad's had a bit of trouble with . . . ' But she'd stalked off by then.

When we got back into the real country again, she didn't want to see anyone, or stay in the villages. All she seemed to be interested in was wild flowers. We should do a book about them, I said. Take a couple of llamas – how she loved those comical-looking beasts – and make an extended trek into the mountains. If there were flowers like these here, who knew what glories lay beyond the farthest peaks? Jean was enthusiastic. Perhaps we wouldn't have to go back to England at all. But no, we must have the best available equipment. She would have to learn about photography – take a course. We should approach some publishers.

If she was up one day, though, she was down the next. 'What's the matter?' I said to her, finally.

'They've given me up.'

'Who has?'

'Doug. And Claire.'

'What d'you mean?'

'I haven't had a letter since San Francisco.'

'I told you about the post. It's . . . ' But there was no reassuring her. She'd been cut out of their lives. It was difficult to know just how to react to this. On the one hand, nothing would have made me happier than to be certain she was right. On the other, I did not like to see her hurt or upset. Privately, I imagined they'd been too lazy to write – too busy, as they would put it. They'd be there for her when she got home, I was quite sure of that, but it was not exactly in my interest to press that view on her. And it might be just the post – I hadn't been exaggerating that much. When a two month-old letter from her mother arrived that had been misaddressed, I pounced on that. 'Are you sure you gave them the right dates?' But that only made her cry.

Most of the time, however, Jean was loving and considerate. I was convinced that it wouldn't take much more for her to agree to marriage, much as she scorned that most Victorian of institutions. 'Why is *that* so important?' she had said more than once. 'Would it make any real difference?'

'To me. Yes.'

'Oh, Ian. You're such an old fuddy-duddy.' As for

telling her what I really thought about Doug and Claire and their Bohemian life-style, any mention of the subject was sure to kindle a furious argument.

We had been travelling two months, had finally left the Huascaran Mountain Range, and were heading for Cuzco, when the rains hit. The first time clouds darkened the skies overhead and the thunder rolled, we were eating our lunch. We did our best to ignore the ominous flashes of lightning and the gathering gloom. But we couldn't ignore the downpour that followed. When it happened again the next day, just at noon, we crawled into the tent – not quite in time. On the third day, we set up the tent before making the sandwiches, and from then on it was capes and plastic bags – over hands and feet – every afternoon; soggy, steaming clothes dripping into the cooking pots every night; and, in the passes, snow. The barefooted Peruvian woman we followed through one pass, protected from the sleet only by the flank of her llama, inhibited Jean's expression of her miseries, but not for long. Nor could I remind her that things were not always pleasant when one was touring, or venture to suggest that had we dawdled less and cycled more, we would be well on our way to Brazil by now. Actually, we would have had to stay somewhere for the three months of the rains. Crossing the Peruvian Gap during the 'dry' season would be damp enough.

However, at all but the worst times, the seasonal difficulties did make for experiences that Jean admitted were unforgettable; whole hillsides molten in mud-flood; valleys hidden among snow peaks blanketed by herds of alpaca. If we were occasionally wakened by torrents where streams had been, by boulders grinding by in the night; if the road we travelled sometimes became a sea of mud, our tent was more than ever our home: a true sanctuary, where a plastic sheet over layers of damp clothing provided unexpected comfort; where being forced to cook inside the tent made for a blissful warmth.

Yet, once we reached the bottom of that last, long descent, she became ecstatic in anticipation of the dry bed, the dry socks, the warm restaurant that would soon be ours. We stayed two extra days in that luxurious haven before taking the train to Lima.

Two weeks later, however, we were back on the road. Our delicate finances did not allow us the comforts of civilization for long; and, once we had collected our replacement equipment, we were ready to go; first to Cuzco, thence to Machu Picchu. That was a sight I had promised Jean ever since our first week together; and rain, even in the rainy season, is not unremitting.

In Lima Jean's mail at last caught up with her. It was as I had said. Most of the letters had been written months ago. They simply hadn't been forwarded. Jean was elated, and though we did not discuss in detail the communications from her friends, I did gather that they were missing her; in fact, that if she didn't hurry up and come home little Sue would have forgotten her.

'Doug still on the dole, then?' I casually remarked.

'If that's what you want to call it.'

'What would you call it?'

'Really, Ian, you're not going to argue that the economic situation's his fault.' I wasn't going to argue anything, I told her. 'What I don't understand is why they haven't received my letters. Not one since we've been here. What must they think?' I let that pass, happy that though the six months were up, there was no talk of cutting our trans-continental tour short.

Our plan was to ride to La Paz, in Bolivia, and make our way from there to the Trans Amazonian Highway through an interconnecting system of roads and waterways. Part of the distance we would travel by canoe. Not that we were going to float down a river in a rubber raft with all mod. cons. It would still be an adventure – one with more than just a fillip of peril in it, too. Obviously, the canoeing part would render invalid any claim to have cycled across the continent. But what did that matter now – what I was counting on was that by the time we reached the east coast of Brazil, Jean and I would be married. If not actually married, committed to it in no uncertain way. But then something happened that changed all our plans.

Chapter Six

Ever since we had arrived in Peru, we had both suffered from occasional bouts of dysentery. It was one of the unpleasantnesses one grew to expect. Admittedly, Jean had had a worse time of it than I: no doctor had inflicted upon me a series of injections the only effect of which was to make it absolutely impossible to use my bicycle seat for the purpose intended. But then it turned out that dysentery was not really the problem. In Urcos, about to leave for La Paz, Jean broke down and was admitted to the British Evangelical Clinic.

'Do you have any plans for the next six weeks or so?' the doctor asked me the following morning when I visited Jean. I gaped at him in disbelief. 'Your companion has hepatitis. Jaundice, that is. Unless, of course, her eyes are naturally yellow.' I must have shown the distress I was feeling for he kindly added: 'Don't look so low, old man. We'll see how she responds to treatment.' And then he was off, white coat flying, sweeping a bevy of nurses along with him.

Jean took the news much better than I. 'Six weeks isn't so very long, Ian. And if he thinks by then I'll be all right, you can go to Lima and arrange about our things.' I dragged myself around Urcos for the next week, utterly miserable; meanwhile Jean was having a fine time. She was making friends with the other patients and was clearly a favourite with the doctor. Also, she was getting better.

In fact, by the end of the week, the doctor had virtually promised us she could leave within another week or so. How my heart sang at that news! When I boarded the train for the 22-hour ride to Lima, I was confident that by the time I returned, Jean would be well enough to start pedalling her way back to strength and full recovery.

I had been in Lima ten days, had purchased all we needed and was just saying goodbye to the staff at the embassy when who should turn up but Jean. She looked terrible. 'What's happened?' I said.

'He's sending me home,' she announced, gloomily. 'Back to England.'

It was actually more to do with her general physical condition than with the disease itself. What she really needed was a good long rest. There was no point in her staying here. What's more, England was a much healthier place in which to recover. It didn't take me long to make up my mind.

'All right,' I said. 'I'll see to our tickets.'

'No, Ian. You mustn't. You have to go on. You can't give it up.'

'Why not?'

'You can't, that's all.' And then she glared at me. I can't describe just how. It was the same look she'd directed at those Peruvian boys who had hurled rocks at us. Her eyes fairly bored into me, so painfully that I finally turned away. 'You're a cyclist, Ian. That's your life. What we were planning to do wasn't the real thing, anyway.' She went on and on. I couldn't up and quit just because she'd been laid low. What's more, if I returned with her to England, what would I do?

I could have answered all her questions if she'd let me. Wait on her. Help her recover. Get a job, I suppose. The hell with all that, I wanted to say. Hadn't I cycled enough? Was I to be strapped to a bicycle seat for the rest of my life? Couldn't I live like other people? And then, all at once, it hit me. She didn't want me to come with her. She didn't love me.

'Ian, dearest. Don't look like that.' She put her arms round me and hugged me to her. 'I'll be there when you've finished. I'll be waiting for you,' she whispered.

There in the embassy foyer we held each other as if we were the only two people in the world. People stopped and stared. But I didn't care. I gripped her all the tighter, as if I could literally hold her back. Yet all the time I knew that she would have to go.

Jaundice had weakened Jean terribly. Yet to me she was more lovely than ever. In fact, there was a quietness, a serenity about her that I had never seen before. She was my Camille, I told her. That she would eventually recover allowed me to indulge my agony to the fullest. For four days I worshipped her. She laughed at my fancy, but took me in her arms.

At last the awful moment came. Jean's plane had been delayed and we had gained a three-hour reprieve – but now its departure was being announced. No, I could not let her go, I told her, clasping her still more tightly in my arms. She made no resistance, and my mind sped through a scenario which had us all the way to the Bolivian border.

Then, gently but firmly, she pushed me away. Her eyes were filled with tears. At the same time, however, she picked up her bag. Her eyes never left mine as she backed away to the gate. Then suddenly she turned. The thread that connected us snapped, and I lost her in the crowd.

A week later I was straining up a steep road to the east of Urcos, heading for the spine of the Andes and the long descent to Puerto Maldonado, the jumping-off spot for the so-called 'Peruvian Gap'. To my knowledge, no one had ever attempted crossing over into Brazil this way before. There was no road, only a trackless wilderness some 200 kilometres wide. I would have to hack my way through dense jungle. What other specific hardships there were, I did not know; for much of the area had not been mapped. I had been told, however, that there were tribes of Indians living in there that still took heads. I knew there would be jaguars, anacondas, piranha fish, deadly spiders, and a rich variety of poisonous insects. What I was particularly not looking forward to meeting was the beautifully-coloured miniature frog, one touch of whose skin brought instant death.

Chapter Seven

A clearing, 40 kilometres north of Puerto Maldonado

Dearest Jean,

I've spoken so much in other letters of 'my aching heart' that I thought I'd give you a bit of a break, solve all our problems, and simply transport you here at once.

There! All snug? Not a bad dinner for the first night out, eh? Considering who's the chef. Or a bad day's ride. Wasn't supposed to be a track, even. So, who's the pessimist? Ride on, I say. Things never as bad as they're cracked up to be. If it's like this tomorrow we'll be at the Rio Manuripe: a third of the way. Should we break out the champagne? What do you mean it's hot here? Like pedalling about in a sauna? Hold on while I write that down.

Your feet cold? So tuck them in, you know where. Only NOT TOO HARD! Mmmm. I could too.

The screen was black with mosquitoes, but it was not their whine that had jerked me rudely awake but the angry bark of a man's voice. It appeared he wanted my blood. He stood there in the track shaking his rifle at me. I had to go! Immediately! He gave me half an hour. If I were still there when he returned, he would shoot.

In order to set up my tent the evening before, I had had to cut a clearing in the eight-foot grass with my machete. Was that it? Was I trespassing? Out there in the jungle? I could have laughed – almost. I ate a handful of raisins, a boiled potato from the night before, and drank some water. No time to make tea. My friend with the gun appeared to be a man of resolve. I did not want to test him further. In less than ten minutes I was off – in a cloud of mosquitoes, wheels spinning on the dew-slicked mud.

It was not the way I would choose to start the day. On the other hand, the track continued to be good. There were other tracks going off to either side, though never any question of which was the main one. It was rolling hill country: high grasses with occasional palms. Hardly the sort of jungle wilderness I had been led to expect.

A missionary in Puerto Maldonado had told me about the road: eighty kilometres, all the way to Mavita, on the Rio Manuripe. After that there was nothing. If I wanted to get to Iberia, where the road picked up again, I would have to fly. This was the true 'Peruvian Gap': an impenetrable jungle of approximately a hundred kilometres. Probably there would be trails, I thought. The day before I had passed several small villages that were unmarked on the map. There might even be a ridable track all the way. I would never have confessed it but all this was somewhat disappointing. I had wanted something truly horrendous to test myself against – something I could count on to fully occupy my mind. I had allowed three months. The longest this could possibly take me, I decided, was three weeks. And if there was indeed a track, I would be in Iberia in a few days.

From Lima, it had taken me six weeks to get to Puerto Maldonado. First the flight to La Paz, to arrange about forwarding my gear. Then the ride to Urcos where Jean's first letters awaited me: one written on the plane, the other the first week she was home. 'You've got your companion in me, Ian,' she had said. 'Sometime in the next two years we'll be off again.' How I treasured those words. And yet . . . she also spoke of how much she was looking forward to seeing 'her dear friends in Ashbury'. Of her illness, and what was being done for it, she wrote not a word. The climb from Urcos to that final pass seemed endless: a pure torture to the lungs. The run to Puerto Maldonado was all down-hill, but it took two weeks; plenty of time to brood and indulge in my own particularly noxious brand of self-pity. But there were two more letters when I arrived, and they carried me forward so blissfully that as I cycled off into the jungle, I was already trying to gauge when would be the earliest I could hope to reach Recife.

Flies swarmed over every part of my body, searching for sweat. Nothing had prepared me for this: not Mt. Huascaran, not the Sahara. Had Jean been with me then she would surely have gone mad. I could not ride fast enough for the wind to take them away. They crawled over me like bees, squirmed into my shorts and nestled themselves in my armpits, even though I kept my elbows pressed to my side. Thank God they did not bite. They were like Australian flies in that respect. But they came in clouds. When I stopped to push my bike through a pool of water or carry it over a fallen tree, so many covered me that I thought of them as my 'hair shirt'.

With the first sign of darkness the flies disappeared — only to be replaced by mosquitoes, hordes of them. Desperately, I looked for a place to set up my tent. Seeing signs of a village coming up, I settled for the first spot, knowing from bitter experience that my tent was a palace compared to anything a village had to offer. No sooner was I settled in, however — I was just in the act of putting a cup of tea to my lips — when I was confronted by a face. 'Brother?' said an old woman from the other side of my bug-blackened screen. I was loath even to answer, but she was not discouraged. 'Brother!' she said again, and gestured imperiously with her arm. With the greatest reluctance I crawled out of my tent, hoping that all she wanted was a cigarette or some chocolate, though I had neither to offer her. She was not a beggar, however. She clasped me in her bony arms and told me to follow her. There seemed no alternative but to obey.

Slapping at the mosquitoes, which did not seem to bother her, I made my way to a rickety-looking bridge. Surely I was not to cross that? But she was adamant. Very cautiously, I climbed out on to the narrow walkway of boards, a rail-less tightrope that served as a path across a foul-looking stream stagnating far below me. I could practically hear the piranha fish clicking their jaws. She gestured me on. Neither looking down nor imperilling my balance by swatting at the blood-sucking swarms, I crept across the bridge in the near dark, one trembling foot in front of the other. With a sudden plunge, I fell into the waiting arms of two men who greeted me with the enthusiasm of long-lost kin. I recalled stories from my youth in which the white man was mistaken for a god – as well as tales of human sacrifice – and reminded myself that whatever the explanation, I had better not make a fuss.

The village of Mavita consisted, as I'd feared, of a dozen or so corrugated tin shacks. Three mangy dogs ushered us in with their yelps, and a scrawny hen hustled her squawking entourage under cover. We waited in front of the least ramshackle hut. Suddenly a door was thrown open and an old woman stepped out. '*Buenas noches, Señor Hibili,*' she cried out. Smiling broadly, she stood aside, indicating that I should enter. 'Brother!' she said, and she too clasped me in an embrace.

It turned out to be the doing of my missionary friend. By sending word that I was a 'brother', he had guaranteed that I would be treated as a special guest. He meant well, of course. Instead of sleeping in the peaceful security of my jungle tent, however, I passed the night on the damp floor of an evil-smelling shack and had to endure the mournful crescendos of 'hymn sing' which drifted endlessly out into the dark.

The river was shedding its early morning mantle of mist as we pushed out across it in the canoe. I could see no break in the bank on the other side, but my friends assured me there was one. The track lay straight ahead. All I had to do was follow it. How long would it take to reach the nearest village, a place called Alerta? Three weeks? No one seemed to have the least idea. People went there. People came back. That was all they knew. As we approached the other side, sure enough a gap opened in the wall of the vegetation. More like a slit, actually, in the fold of a curtain; but it proved to be wide enough to allow me to slip in. Instantly, I felt claustrophobic. The tendrils of the vines seemed to reach down and clutch at me. Two steps away from the river it was twilight, though what sun did filter through the dense canopy overhead turned the leaves into mirrors. In the midst of darkness, I was blinded by light.

Cougars, or was it jaguars, abounded in places like this, I had been told. Invisible, they stretched out along the lower branches of trees, quietly waiting to pounce upon the unwary. Everywhere around me I seemed to see their luminous eyes. Behind every leaf I visualized a paw hanging, claws extended. Once I was away from the river the danger of meeting an anaconda would be much less, but that was hardly a consolation. They, too, draped themselves over the lower branches. And so closely did their smoothly-looped bodies resemble the limbs of trees that the jungle traveller sometimes mistook one for the other. I shivered as I recalled a gruesome story about a party of soldiers, one of whom grabbed a vine for support as he lowered himself to the riverbank. Not a vine, as it turned out, but a forty-foot anaconda that coiled itself around him instantly in foot-thick loops. Before the others could reach him, three of his ribs were broken. After they cut the coils away, they were amazed to see that the severed pieces writhed as if they still had strength.

Very slowly, I pushed my way along the narrow trail, trying hard to touch nothing. First there was a maze of elephant's-ear, then a massive tree whose root arched out from its trunk. The trail wound around and between smooth-barked trees and across spongy acres of forest floor where there was virtually no light. Then it began to climb. The trees diminished in size, the undergrowth thickened; and soon I was pushing through stands of palmettos, clumps of exotic-looking tropical plants, and thickets of bamboo. The track disappeared. Then I found it again. I was sweating profusely by then and my progress was painfully slow, for I had to ferry my things. I would break or cut my way through a patch, return, unstrap the panniers and carry them forward, then make another trip with the bike. In some places I had to lift my unwieldy cycle up over my shoulders to get it through.

I kept expecting the track to open up. Instead it disappeared. Finally, after three hours of futile bush-whacking, I admitted defeat. I would have to go back to the river, swim across to the village – I shuddered at the thought – and find out where I had gone wrong. What a fool not to have had them make me a map! I had a painful blister on the palm of my right hand, and I was exhausted. Slumped on the ground, propped up by my rucksack, I tried to take consolation in the fact that there were amazingly few bugs. 'Too thick even for those blighters,' I said aloud. Three hours out and already I was talking to myself!

Suddenly I sprang up. What was that? It sounded as if a couple of elephants were crashing about. And then, through the palmettos, I saw the startled face of an Indian. 'Hello,' I said. There was another Indian behind him. He pushed a branch to one side, and we stared at each other for a minute in mutual surprise. I waved my arm in a circle and mouthed the name 'Alerta' in a variety of accents, pointing my hand this way and that.

'Alerta!' one of them said, finally. Instantly, he dropped down on his haunches and drew a sketch map in a patch of mud. I must go back to the river crossing. I had taken the wrong fork. I should have gone to the right. 'Impossible,' I said, indicating my meaning with a frown and a shake of the head. No, he insisted, striking the mud with a stick. There was a good trail. In half an hour we were back at the river bank.

The Indian was parting the bushes so I could see that indeed there was a patch of well-worn earth leading off into a thicket. I took a few tentative steps and found that the branches parted easily. On the ground in front of me were the imprints of bare feet. I pointed them out to my companions. A party of ten. They counted it out on their fingers. A pity – they had passed that way only that morning. I could have joined them. Confident now, if disappointed, I thanked them as best I could and pushed on. In a matter of twenty minutes or so, the undergrowth gave way to a forest of widely-spaced trees, the huge boles of which disappeared upward into a vast canopy of branches; and I was actually able to ride. As my eyes became accustomed to the darkness, I began to ride more quickly. There was suddenly a sense of space – like cycling across the carpet of some vast hall. It was cool and still. The forest held a peace that was almost cathedral-like.

For the next two days I rode, and walked, and pushed, and rode again, until at last I staggered into the tiny village of Alerta. The distance, as near as I could estimate, was 35 kilometres. Except for that first section, there was never any question of being lost. The anacondas and the cougars had passed me by. I had seen no sign of the deadly-skinned toad, and the natives I had come upon were friendly. I was a mass of scratches and cuts, my shorts were torn and my shirt was no more than a filthy rag; but I had made my way through a third of the impassable 'Peruvian Gap'. Though ready for a rest, I felt uncommonly gratified.

Chapter Eight

'You must go back,' the soldier said, handing me my passport. The next morning I called upon the garrison commander: a Sergeant Mendez. He stood there, very stiff and proud, a crescent of sweat darkening the underarms of his wilted khaki uniform. After considering the matter, he informed me with Olympian detachment that I would have to return to Puerto Maldonado.

I was nonplussed.

'No exit visa.' He looked at me as if I were a naughty child.

'I can't get one here?' He smiled and shook his head. 'Puerto Maldonado,' he said and gestured for me to leave.

I begged. I pleaded. I told him all the places I had been, all the troubles I had endured.

'You are going to Brazil?' he said, finally. 'On that?'

I nodded my head. 'All the way to the Atlantic.'

'And you have come from Lima? On a bicycle?' The soldier standing at attention beside him, his magnificent moustachios curling up to frame his eyes, allowed himself the trace of a smile. Instantly, the commander wheeled toward him. '*Idiota!*' he shouted. The corners of the moustache visibly drooped as the soldier received the most thorough dressing-down I have ever witnessed. When the man was utterly cowed, practically sinking through the floor, Sergeant Mendez turned from him in disgust. My turn now, I thought. With infinite disdain the Napoleon of Alerta picked up my passport, held it to the light, flipped through its pages, seemed on the verge of tossing it away, and then slapped it down upon the desk. 'You may continue,' he said.

'*Gracias*,' I replied.

'*Buenos dias*,' he answered. He handed me my passport and added: 'Señor, the plane for San Lorenzo leaves in the morning.' Holding up his hand, as if to forestall further discussion, he continued: 'There is no other way.'

Half an hour later I was conversing with a group of villagers, all of whom seemed to share the Sergeant's view. Air service to San Lorenzo was free. It was provided by the military. No one thought of going any other way. Mavita, Iberia, Puerto Maldonado; I could fly to any of these places if I wished. Every little village in the jungle had its airstrip. It was cheaper for the government to do this than to build roads.

But what if one *wants* to walk? I said. Smiles. Much shaking of the head. Señor Hibell is perhaps a nut gatherer? He works for the rubber company as a tapper of trees? Uncontrolled laughter at this suggestion. So there were trails, I said. People did live out there. One or two. But the trails went from one rubber or Brazil nut tree to another. I might walk for two or three days, only to end up where I had begun.

'But there must be a trail to San Lorenzo, too.' Yes. One voice at last admitted to that. However, I would never find it. Not without a guide.

For three days I waited for a man named Pedro to show up. He was the only one, apparently, who knew the area. Finally I decided to go on without him. I had discovered that there were at least two people living out there. There was a nut gatherer, Raphael, whose hut was less than a day's walk from the village. The legendary Simplicio lived further on. He never emerged from the jungle now, but Raphael might be able to direct me to him, *if* I found Raphael. Simplicio was a rubber tapper. He took his wares out by canoe. A year ago he had been badly mauled by a jaguar, his dog torn apart. But he'd crawled back to his hut and when Raphael found him a month later, his leg was well on its way to being healed. If I reached Simplicio's I would be all right, everyone agreed. He would surely be able to direct me to San Lorenzo.

Armed with a sketch map, I crossed the river on a crude bamboo raft and made my way towards a wide cut in the bank. It looked like a vehicle track. I stared at my companion in disbelief. 'It does not go far,' he said, laughing. 'Once they tried to build a road here. The track you must take goes off to the right two hundred metres beyond the four-kilometre post.' I thanked him, but determined to explore the road for myself. It seemed incredible that nobody had even mentioned its existence.

It was a road all right, with ruts that could only have been made by heavy machinery. A grassy strip was running down the middle of it, but all that meant was that it was not getting much use. And why would it, considering that there was no bridge and no road on the other bank? In less than a minute, I was buzzing along in high gear, humming to myself and picturing my triumphal re-entry into civilization. Perhaps I would be in San Lorenzo that very evening, even Iberia, by my calculations no more than 70 kilometres away. The grasses of the savanna swept past me in a blur of green and I was just beginning to wonder whether or not there was a chance I would be able to pick up mail tomorrow, when the road came to an abrupt end. Though my guide had warned me, I couldn't believe it. Where were the bulldozers? Where were the men? They could not have vanished into thin air. I decided to explore further. An hour later, and for the second time in a week, I admitted defeat. I was back at square one, looking for the four-kilometre post.

The track, when I finally found it, was so narrow and so bad that I could not even wheel my bike along it.

But worse than that was the heat. The slightest effort produced cascades of sweat. So I stripped off all my clothes – went native at last. Fortunately, there were no insects. Had there been, I would have gone berserk. It was more a pig-run than a track, the trees so close together in places that I would have to press between them sideways. And every few metres, it seemed, I was either climbing over or crawling under one. I ploughed through muddy hollows reminiscent of the Atrato, and crossed single-log bridges where one false step would have plunged me deep into a bottomless morass. Many a time I wasted precious energy hacking my way through the undergrowth only to discover afterwards that the track went around.

It was about noon when I heard something crashing through the underbrush ahead of me. Jaguar! was my first thought. I dropped my panniers and fled back to where I had left my machete. I had just pulled on my shorts and turned to face the enemy, weapon raised, when the bushes parted and a monstrous sack wobbled into view. Underneath, an ancient face peered up at me. And then came an equally heavily-laden, and even more bent-over, old woman. '*Buenos dias*,' the old man said. Like strangers thrown together at a bus depot, we sat there, exchanging bits of information. They were Brazil nut gatherers and would be back this way in three or four days with their empty sacks. I said I trusted that I would not still be there by then. Shortly after that they departed – before I had thought to ask them about the track ahead.

There was little I could do but plunge on, through thickets so dense that I couldn't believe those frail old people with their gigantic burdens could possibly have penetrated them; through pools of water that reached above my knees; around and in between the trunks and roots of countless trees. But towards evening I was rewarded. I came to a clearing, in the middle of which was a small hut. Two young men and a woman were chipping away at a pile of Brazil nuts, down by a stream. 'Raphael?' I called out, and one of the men stood up and shook my hand.

I bathed in the cool, clear water; and, after a 'feast' of yams and coffee, slept the sleep of the just. Simplicio's hut was a mere four hours away. The only thing I had to remember was not to take the track that branched off to the right just before I reached the end, unless I wished to go to Bolivia. It was plain sailing. All I had to do was keep straight ahead.

I had hardly got out of sight of Raphael's clearing the next morning when I came to a fork in the track; not a fork exactly – another track that came in from the right, joined the one I was following, and then branched off it to the left. Or was that the main track, and the one going to the right the branch? What to do? I took the left one and followed it for a way. It seemed to go further and further to the left. I came back and took the other. I went more or less straight. For perhaps 400 metres I pushed my way along a track that became steadily worse. I was having to ferry my things now. I was on the verge of retracing my steps when I came to another 'crossroad'. This time one track was clearly better than the other. For 200 metres I could actually ride. Then it, too, petered out, and suddenly it turned into three distinctly different trails, none of which looked as if anyone had passed over it in weeks. I took the middle one. It was crossed at an angle by another a little further on. I stayed with it. It improved. I came to yet another intersecting track, unquestionably used recently but going off at right angles. I kept straight on. And then I reached a clearing and noticed that the sun was in the wrong place entirely. I got out my compass, walked back to the crossroad and took the other track. From then on I consulted the compass at every crossing.

I could not, of course, use the compass to guide me directly through the jungle. All day I plodded: four hours, six hours, eight hours. I had made a hundred decisions by then, any one of which might have led me hopelessly off. Yet, for some reason, I felt I was on the right track. Why, then, had I not reached Simplicio's? Because I was progressing so slowly. Should I hurry on, then, unencumbered? The idea was too tempting to resist.

For the next half hour I actually ran. The wind cooled me, or seemed to, and I gloried in my freedom, the lightness of my body. I got off for a while on to what proved to be an ancient trail, long disused. There was a section where I had to press through waist-high grass; and then, just as my time was almost up, I came to a distinct fork in the track. This must be it, I thought. The right one goes to Bolivia, the other to Simplicio's. I turned to the left and soon broke into a run again. There was little more than an hour of daylight; yet I was so near, too near to go back.

I ran on – and on. Twilight began to fall. I shivered in the sudden gloom. Trying not to think about what it would be like to spend the night out there without my tent, I plunged on. I had to reach Simplicio's soon.

Darkness comes quickly in the jungle. All at once I could not make out the trail. Was that the cry of a howler monkey? Or a jaguar? Surprisingly quiet and uninhabited during the day, the jungle is a battleground at night: the pursuer and the pursued – the broken twig, the padding step; every cry equally terrifying. One learns to ignore all this within the safety of a tent.

I barked my shin on a fallen tree and leapt off into the darkness, hoping not to disturb the snake that might be lodging there, just on the other side. Then I was in another clearing and the track seemed to end. But no. It went to the right and to the left. Was this the main track? If so, one way led back to Raphael's, the other to Simplicio's. But which was which? I made what I hoped was my last decision. I turned to the right. In less than a minute there it was! a hut, a fire, a man bent over it leaning heavily on a stick. 'Simplicio?' I called out. The man grunted.

I collapsed at his feet.

Chapter Nine

I'd been sleeping heavily, bone weary from my third day's struggle with the jungle. After spending most of the day going back for my gear, I had made camp only a kilometre or so beyond Simplicio's hut. What had woken me with such a start? The chattering of a monkey scampering back into its arboreal nest? I lit a candle, thinking that whatever it was would be scared off by the light. The jungle was silent. I let myself fall back on to my sleeping bag, and my eyes rested on the ceiling. What I saw made my body go rigid with fright. There, outlined on the fly sheet, was a gigantic spider. Its monstrous body covered the peak of the tent, its hairy legs hung down both sides half way to the floor. And then the candle flickered and went out.

Trembling, frantic, expecting at any moment to feel those spidery arms, I fumbled with a match. One, two, the third flared into life, and I raised the lit candle above me, as if to propitiate some pagan god. And then I realized what it was. Above the netting was a large spider – a very large one, indeed: almost the size of my palm. I could see its mouth opening and closing in anticipation. But what I had seen was its magnified image projected on the fly sheet above – a trick of the light. I banged a shoe at the loathsome creature and it scuttled away. Just as I did so, however, I felt a sting on my leg. I held the candle lower, dreading what I might see. Nothing. The screen door was closed. The rest of the netting secure. Whatever it was must be tiny – but it was also poisonous. And somewhere in here.

A preliminary search revealed nothing. What I had to do was move everything from one side of the tent to the other; examine each item carefully, taking care not to be bitten again. Half an hour later I had done just that – and found nothing. Just as I was about to start all over again, I noticed a flicker of movement on one of my shoes.

Cautiously, I picked it up. Locating my toothbrush, I delicately jabbed at the insides. No signs of life. About to put that shoe down and examine its mate, I gave the toothbrush a last twirl and out popped a small, furry spider no larger than the button on my shirt. He balanced there, on the tongue of my shoe, and threatened me with his tiny claws. So this was it, this insignificant creature. Raising the other shoe, I gauged the distance. But then I paused. There was something in the pluckiness of my tiny antagonist that I could not help but admire. Lowering my weapon, I unzipped the screen and brushed my would-be assassin out into the night. It was only later that the thought occurred to me that this creature might not be the real offender, that I should have combed everything a second time. But by then it was almost daylight.

I woke up in a terrible sweat, my whole leg throbbing and stiff and impossible to touch. I made a crude compress with a water-soaked shirt and fanned it for a while, but I doubt if that helped much. Then I must have passed into unconsciousness again, for the next thing I remember it was very hot and full daylight.

Scrambling around, I found the leftover rice from the night before, ate a few handfuls, and drank some mouthfuls of water. I tried to stand, but I could not. 'Jean?' I called out. No answer. I had to catch up with her, or she would get too far ahead. Or was she waiting for me, just out there? Hiding? It was her way to get me going. She had comforted me during the night. Her loving eyes had gazed into my own, and given me strength. Her hands had cooled my brow. It was her voice – so tender, so warm – that had lulled me to sleep. When I woke up in the darkness, choking, unable to catch my breath, it was she who held me, she who told me over and over again that I had nothing to fear. Of course, I would reach San Lorenzo. She would help me. It was absurd and very wrong of me to think that I might die.

As quickly as I could, I packed up my things. Then,

steeling myself for the supreme effort, I crept out of the door of my tent. The pain was excruciating, but once I had loaded the bike – how I did that I will never know – I could let the frame carry part of my weight. Leaning on this crutch, crying out with pain each time my foot touched the ground, I made my way along the trail. In the shadows at the turn of the trail, I thought I caught glimpses of her. I called out, but she would not respond. I pushed harder, hoping to reach her. But always she remained just ahead.

All day long she glided before me. Sometimes the sunlight danced around her. Sometimes she hid in the shadows. I tried to make her answer me, but she only smiled. When there was a choice of which way to go, I would look for her, and there she would be. Late in the afternoon we reached a spot where a large tree had fallen across the path and been cut through. Another track branched off to the right, however, and we took that. Soon the jungle began to thin out. The trail became flat. And then, suddenly, there was sand ahead and beyond that the river. I crawled out on to the sand, pulling myself forward with my arms, pushing with my good leg. The effort was torture, but I knew that in a minute I would see the huts of San Lorenzo dotting the opposite shore. The blood pounded in my temples. And then I saw no more.

When I regained consciousness, it was night. I lay there, listening to the river and the wind in the trees. Surely someone would find me. And then I blacked out again.

The moon was high when I woke up. My heart was racing. Jean and I had been walking the streets of Lima and were just returning to our hotel. We had our arms around each other, and Jean was laughing; for in order to get through the door, we would have to untangle ourselves. We stood there, each one unwilling to make the first move; and then, finally, I took my arm from around her waist. To my horror she began to disappear. She grew dimmer and dimmer – and at last, with a stricken look, she was gone.

'Jean!' I stretched out both my arms, sweeping the sand. 'You fool,' I said to myself. I was alone, and ill, and lost; and I knew it. Crawling back to where I had left my bicycle, I gulped down several sips of water, opened a packet of crackers, found the peanut butter and dug into it with my fingers. Ravenously, I ate; then drank some more. Leaning against my rucksack afterwards, I realized that my brow was cool and dry, my mind clear. I examined my leg, and did not cry out from the pain. Gingerly, I explored the tender part – about the size and consistency of a golf ball. I could bend it, too, a bit. Arranging myself more comfortably, I thanked God that I seemed to be on the mend and instantly fell into a deep sleep. When I awoke the next morning, I felt like a new man.

On the opposite river bank, there was nothing but an unbroken canopy of green: no boats, no paths, no footprints on the sand. I pushed back along the trail toward the cut-through log I dimly remembered having seen. Surely no one would take the trouble to do that unless the track led somewhere. That should have been obvious to me the day before, but most of that day was a blur.

The other trail was clearly the main one. I could even ride it, occasionally. Shortly before noon I heard what sounded like a party going on up ahead: laughter, loud talking. Could that actually be a baby crying? All at once a soldier, brandishing a rifle, practically bumped into me. He aimed the weapon and would have fired, perhaps, had I not called out in alarm. There was a second soldier, four men in all; two women, and a baby. They were on their way to Alerta, had left San Lorenzo that morning. In a few hours I would be there. But how was it I went through these forests unarmed? They shook their heads in disbelief. Even the Indians, who had lived here all their lives, never went into the jungle unarmed. Was I not afraid of snakes, not to mention jaguars? Snakes? Yes, I had seen one coiled on the path in front of me. I had stepped around it. There had been occasional snake-like flickerings in the undergrowth. As for jaguars, I had heard them, that was all. Heard them – one of the men laughed, and then shuddered. Might I continue to be as well-protected in the future. We parted, and I hurried on along a track that got better and better. Soon I was riding. Jungle trees and bushes gave way to tall grasses. The ground became level. Pools of water alternated with marsh grass. There were exotic-looking plants, covered with heavy red flowers. And then the path turned to sand and there, along the opposite river bank, were the huts and boats and fires of San Lorenzo.

A day's rest and I was ready for the final push. The pain in my leg had subsided and all that was left was a hard red swelling on my left upper thigh. Iberia? Everyone pointed up the river. Several boatmen immediately began haggling over the price. 'The trail. Where is the track?' I said. There was one, but since everyone went by boat, it was little used. Only when they were finally convinced I was serious did a police officer lead me to the back of the village and point it out. He had to literally part the branches.

That day is one that still haunts me: a track, then nothing; a nightmare, repeated again and again. My own passage, of course, left tell-tale marks: a footprint here, a scraped bit of moss there, a twig dangling from its parent branch. On my way back for my gear I would journey from island to island of familiarity. But by nightfall, I had covered only a few kilometres. The next day, however, the track became quite good. By noon I was riding most of the time. And then, suddenly, I was there. Fifty kilometres? For once the estimate failed in my favour. More like twenty-five. I could hardly believe it, but my jungle walk was over.

Iberia is a small city, a centre of commerce. I was the first in the queue at the post office the next morning.

'There must be more,' I said. The woman looked at me angrily, for I had already made her go through the mail twice. Not one letter from Jean? Impossible! And then thoughts I had been fighting back ever since Jean left rose to the surface and overwhelmed me. She didn't care. She had never truly cared. I had been a necessary companion, nothing more. Now that she was back with her 'family' in Ashbury, she had no more time for me.

Mechanically, I read Josh's letter over for the third time. There was a writer trying to get in touch with me from the States. Life in Seattle churned away at about the same rate. He was putting on weight, but taking it off again on long, lovely rides into the mountains. There was a girl who'd become rather special to him.

'There is something,' the woman said. I ran over. The flicker of hope died as she handed me the package of spare parts and extra gear that I had shipped ahead from Urcos. 'It will never get there,' several people had said. But in fact it had taken only four days.

The following day I rode to Inapari, a distance of 70 kilometres. There was no letter from Jean for me there either. When they stamped me through at the border and told me I was fortunate not to be sent all the way back to Puerto Maldonado, I felt no emotion. The next place I could hope for mail was Porto Velho, a thousand kilometres away.

Chapter Ten

I had thought that Brazil would be easy. Soaked in sweat, I panted up hills while trucks and cars plastered me with dust. The mosquitoes that rose from the swamps in the evening blackened the sky and all but devoured me before I reached the sanctuary of my tent. But what did it matter? The very ugliness that surrounded me – the roadside huts grouped around the one petrol pump; the acrid, burning forest-fields – gratified my soul. The one glorious moment of the day, when I would dive naked, still dripping from my bath into the safety of the tent; the time for reading, writing letters, eating my main meals – this became the most hellish period of all; for then I would conjure up nightmare visions of Jean: on the lap of that film director she had been so taken with on the flight from Lima; snuggled up against the attractive Irishman who had taken his place in Los Angeles. And then there was Doug, with Colin lecherous in the background. I saw her in his arms, her face flushed with passion: body squirming, mouth tensed, eyes suddenly ablaze.

It was dark in the tent by 6 o'clock; for twelve hours I had to lie there and battle with the demons. It was bad enough when I was conscious. But when at last I fell asleep there was no reining them in. In my saner moments, I wondered why I was so certain that Jean had deceived me. But those were daylight thoughts. Most of the time I wallowed in the emotions that had led me to write that curt letter from Inapari:

Inapari, June 19

Dear Jean:

Your silence speaks louder than any words. I do not blame you. I have known, in fact, always, that I felt far more strongly for you than ever you did for me. But I had hoped that we were more than just travelling companions. Not to have sent me any message in all this time was cruel. It has been more than two months, and I do not even know if you are well. How I regret now not having flown back with you. And yet to have been dropped after our return would have been still worse. Was that why you urged me on with such passion? The pain is more than I can bear.

Ian

There was a large packet of letters for me in Porto Velho: Jean, Jean, Mum, Jean again. At least that many more. My heart pounding, I walked across the street to a bench in the local square. Six of the letters were from Jean. I arranged them by order of their postmarks: Puerto Maldonado, June 3rd; another forwarded from there, the date too badly smudged to make out; Porto Velho, July 13, 15, 22, 28. I opened the July 28th one with trembling fingers.

> *My dearest love,*
> *Your letter from Inapari, dated June 19, has just reached me. It is ridiculously late at night and ridiculously exhausted as I am, I cannot rest until I have spoken my heart out to you. The utter let-down that you felt at no mail from me either in Iberia or Inapari, that it made you unable to write more than a few lines – I know what that means, and sitting here all these weeks later, I cannot alleviate the pain.*
>
> *Ian, my darling, I wrote maybe 4 letters to Iberia and at least 7 to Inapari – all in plenty of time for them to reach you. What ugly stroke of fate made them go astray I cannot imagine, only that the intensity of feeling I have for you has been twisted to look like neglect. Ian, I have one main thing to say to you. I dearly love you, and would give anything to have you hear me say so.*

A large woman with a baby plopped down on the bench beside me. I smiled at her, foolishly.

> *You have no idea the tenderness and love that I want to share with you again. So for me to know that you doubt that makes me feel sick and wobbly inside. I really want to cry – not for myself, because I know that it is all right, but for the unnecessary pain you have to bear until maybe this finds you.*

I dropped the letter into my lap. In the past few moments weeks of agony had melted away, and a warm glow suffused me. The pigeons waddling on the pavement, the old man with his stick across the way, the two young girls whispering together on the bench to my right; all this was so charming: so full of grace, so vibrant with life. The woman next to me made signs that I should move. A man – her husband? – stood above me. Their bench? Certainly. I went off and sat down on a nearby kerb.

Dear Jean. I could see her so clearly: cross-legged, eyes scrunched up to make those furrowy, little lines; chewing on the end of her pen. I all but reached out my hand. Darling gipsy. My love . . .

> *I'm looking for somewhere better to live, out of Ashbury, that can be a home for you. Wherever I am, Ian, you will always belong – free to come and go as you need. I'll be there, waiting for you, as solid as a rock.*

I laughed out loud. Didn't she know what a home-body I was prepared to be? There'd be a bit of a garden, I was sure. Away from it all, but not too far. But what had happened to make her want to get away from Doug and Claire? I was almost too anxious to ask.

I tore open the next letter. And there it was. She was afraid of falling under his influence again. 'I hid nothing from Doug about us, though I didn't tell him much, just that it is beautiful, and as natural and inevitable as the snow on the mountain tops.' He must have been furious, I thought, feeling intensely pleased. Doug and Claire had had another baby, she went on to say. He was turning into quite the family man.

Was it over, then? Could I stop thinking about it? That first night at Ragged Point. Afterwards, she'd been in tears. 'What is it, Jean?' I'd begged her. And finally she'd confessed how guilty she felt. She'd broken faith, she said. And after only three weeks. 'Broken faith with whom?'

'With Doug.'

'I thought you said that was over?'

'It is. It's just that I promised myself not to get involved.'

'What's that got to do with him?'

'He told me I wouldn't be able to.'

'But he urged you to come.'

'I know.' And then she started to cry all over again.

Her letters were filled with such love: 'Yes, Ian, a home-coming. I'll climb into bed beside you, and you'll hold me and make love to me, and I'll curl up in the crook of your arm again, and be there when you wake up.' This was the letter I should have received in Inapari! There was more, much more. I read everything over again, slowly, savouring every little bit.

I spent most of the rest of the day writing to her, trying to make her understand the reasons for my former doubts, pouring out my love. If only I could have flown to her side! But I was doing this for both of us. What I saw and experienced, even the worst parts, she had to share. The quicker I rode on the sooner I would be there. But that was just the trouble. For, before I could go on, I had to go 500 kilometres in the opposite direction – to the twin city of Guajara-Mirim on the river border of Bolivia and Brazil, to pick up a package of spares I had had shipped there from La Paz. Also, I had run out of money. I had my bus fare, and enough to keep me in food for a few days; but no one would cash my travellers' cheques. When I entered Brazil I had wired the British Embassy in Brasilia requesting that they send a money order to me in Porto Velho, but they hadn't. I wired them again, then prepared to take the night bus to Guajara-Mirim.

The enforced delay would serve my purpose in one way. My spider bite had been acting up again. Each evening, for the past fortnight, I had been forced to drain out the pus. What my leg really needed was a rest. But time was running out: in six weeks the rainy season would begin. Also, my enthusiasm for the journey had reached a new low – I had just heard that a German cyclist, a mere boy, had completed the ride from Belém to the end of the Trans-Amazonian Highway in Peru. I knew that I could not give up now, but never had I wanted to so much.

Chapter Eleven

Because of a national holiday, the British Embassy in La Paz was closed, and when I finally got through to them on the following Monday they told me that the nearest place to air freight my spares would be Riberalta, another hundred kilometres by bus beyond Guajara-Mirim. 'They should be there by Thursday,' a cheery British voice explained. By Thursday I might well be dead from starvation, but I didn't tell him that.

'A beautiful ride, Señor. You must certainly plan to go by day,' said the man in the bus depot. Wasn't there anywhere I could cash a traveller's cheque? I asked. He gave it some thought. '*Momento*,' he said, and disappeared into the back office. He returned almost instantly, wreathed in smiles. There was a certain man, an Italian, who, for a consideration, would be able to cash twenty dollars. What sort of consideration? I queried. '*Por favor. Amigo.*'

I had to be driven out to the man's house. There was much examination of documents and signatures. The 'consideration' proved to be a hefty fifty per cent, but at least the remainder would purchase my round trip bus ticket, and I would have a few dollars left over to keep me from fainting in the streets.

For the past three days I had been living the life of a vagrant. Camped on the edge of town, in a swampy section near the river, I would pack up my tent each morning and walk up the hill to the central plaza. While my tent dried in the sun, I sat in a nearby restaurant eating bread and drinking coffee and trying to give the impression that this was the way I chose to spend my days. I wrote in my notebook. I made friends with the waiters. I lingered in the drugstore where a motherly-looking proprietress acknowledged my distress by smothering me with concerned inquiries and an occasional chocolate. About 4 p.m. I returned to my mosquito-infested campsite where I wrote long letters to Jean and tried to ignore my mounting pangs of hunger.

Wednesday night I took the bus to Ribcralta. My spares were there. On the way back to Guajara-Mirim (the ride was indeed a beautiful one), my travelling companion took pity on me and offered to share his bread and cheese – and meat and wine. The next morning I checked through customs on my way up the hill, then prepared to spend the day as usual while waiting for the night bus to Porto Velho. I had just laid out my tent.

'You may not dry your tent here!' snapped the small but surly official. He was flanked by two soldiers.

'Why not?'

'It is against the rules.'

'All right,' I said. 'If you say so.' Never argue. Never ask questions. I had been through all this in La Paz. If they got you to the police station, they would plant drugs on you and you might be in jail for months. There I had escaped only because the 'soldiers' were in plain clothes, and I had bluffed my way out with a demand to see the British consul. I took the tent off the bench and began to fold it.

'You come with us!' growled the official.

'Now?' I said, looking around for a way to flee.

'Yes. You come now!' And with that the soldiers grabbed me.

I am not a large man, nor particularly strong. But

occasionally something happens that shoots my adrenalin level up about a thousand per cent. 'You can't do this!' I yelled and wrenched myself free. 'I'm a British subject!'

By this time a small crowd had gathered, expecting entertainment. 'We have our orders!' said the officer, somewhat taken aback. I started to make a run for it, but they were on me at once. Suddenly, a familiar voice was screaming 'Peeg!' It was my protectress from the drugstore, and in awe I watched her as she pushed her way to the front of the crowd and accosted the astonished officer. Her eyes flamed. 'Peeg!' she screeched again. 'Imbecile! Beast! How dare you attack this man!' The officer cowered in submission. The crowd was ecstatic. This usually benign woman – who was fully six inches taller than the official representative of Bolivian justice – was an Amazon, a tigress in her wrath. Now he tried to convey innocence: no harm was meant. But his support unit had disappeared. 'Follow me!' she commanded, and flicking the officer to one side as if he were so much rubbish, she picked up my box of spares. I grabbed the tent and my rucksack, and triumphantly we made our way across the street to the drugstore, the crowd dancing after us, shouting and flinging hats into the air.

'*Gracias*,' I said, and it was heartfelt. She shrugged her massive shoulders and spat in the direction of the door. Then she planted herself squarely behind the counter. I peered cautiously out of the window. The crowd was still milling about, but the soldiers were gone. Across the street was a 'taxi stand', a line of manned motor bikes; room for one passenger only. Now was my chance. I shouted another '*gracias*' and tore out into the street. 'The river – fast!' I yelled, and we lurched off. People were crossing in front of us from every direction. If only I could make him go faster! I leaned forward, pushing with my weight.

'Hurry! Hurry!'

'Stop!' shouted a voice.

Out of the corner of my eye, I could see a soldier approaching. More people were meandering in front of us. If only they realized my predicament! A block from the boat landing, a terrific traffic jam brought us to a complete stop. I jumped off the bike, ready to run for it. But before I could make a move a soldier had me by the arm.

'No!' I cried. 'I must go through customs!' He hesitated. 'Right there, across the street! I must go now.' I tugged at my arm. The soldier looked at the building, then at me. Then he released his grip. What did this mean? Was he really going to let me go? Edging away from him, I slipped through the crowd, expecting at any minute to feel his hand on my shoulder. Across the street, I turned to see what he was doing. He was running crab-like up the hill. Of course! He needed reinforcements. In another instant, he had disappeared and I was charging full speed toward the quay. I hurdled a low wall, plunged recklessly down a steep bank, knocking into a woman and spilling a whole load of baskets; and there I was. I flung myself wildly on to the nearest boat, pushed through boxes and baskets to the bow, and fell on my face. Panting and trembling, I dared not look up. Presently, however, I caught a glimpse of a sandalled foot – with huge, calloused toes – no more than a few inches from my head. I shut my eyes. When I opened them again, there was another pair of sandalled feet next to the originals – of a slightly more attractive shape and texture; and above them the hem of a skirt. Protection! The nearest thing to bliss I'd experienced in some time.

A few minutes later we were off. I could feel a breeze on my neck and hear the lapping of the waves. Pulling myself up on one elbow, I risked a glance at the shore. No soldiers. Was I safe at last? At that moment our motor coughed, then lapsed into silence. We were perhaps forty metres from the shore. I buried my head again, trembling as before. This time there was no hope. In a minute . . .

But we started up again. The torture was to be continued. The river was about a mile wide. It would take a good twenty minutes for this decrepit craft to make it across. I perked up again. Still no signs of military life on the shore. Ahead of us was a large island. I would feel some peace only when we were around that.

Suddenly, to the accompaniment of much tooting and rocking of the boat, the sandalled passengers at my side lurched backwards and almost fell on top of me. A wave flipped into my face, then another. The smell from the bilge was making me sick. Looming up, no more than a dozen metres away, was the wall of a passing ferry – much too close for comfort. The dirty canvas canopy above our heads, ripped in several places, flapped noisily as the wind picked up. The ship passed. And then I heard the sound of a motor roaring into life and saw a police boat pushing out from shore. It was an air-boat, capable of 50 m.p.h. And it was heading straight for us.

I threw myself flat on the floor. If only the woman would cover me with her skirt. I could hear the motor getting louder and louder. '*Mr Hibell? You are under arrest!*' The voice was as clear in my mind as the stomp of the boots and the click, clack, click of the loading rifles. I had only seconds now. Should I roll overboard? Brave the piranhas and the crocs, the currents, the outboards, the bullets whizzing in spectacular patterns about my matted head? I peered out, trying to gauge the distance, meanwhile inching backwards under the seat. The sound of the air-boat was deafening. I braced myself. And then, mercy of mercies, it began to diminish. I looked up just in time to see it round our bow and go charging off into the distance. '*Imbecilio!*' shouted our boatman as we pitched back and forth, dangerously, in its wake. I grabbed the leg of the large-toed man to prevent myself from sliding. 'Fool! What you do?' He shook me off. I spluttered as a wave broke over my head. I was up against the gunnel, now, gasping like some monstrous blow-fish; but beside myself with joy. How marvellous to be lying here, huddled safely in the bilge; rocking back and forth in this frail, unreliable, pathetic excuse for a boat. I smiled broadly at the sandalled couple, whose faces I saw now for the first time. The woman looked at me with considerable disdain. '*Mal de mer*,' I explained, twisting my expression into something appropriately pathetic. But she remained unmoved.

We were rounding the island. Boats of all shapes and sizes plied their way between the twin cities, looking from here like mirror reflections, sparkling in the sun. A raucous flock of parrots took a turn round the boat and disappeared into the dense canopy of the jungle. How good it was to be alive.

Chapter Twelve

Back in Port Velho, through the aid of a cycling enthusiast at the British Embassy, I was finally wired some money. But I couldn't leave yet, for I had to have an operation. The sore in my leg was worse; the infected part had to be cut out. After that there would be a period of recuperation. 'How long?' I asked the doctor.

'Two to four weeks.'

I groaned. It was now August 15th. The rains were due to start in early September. Yet nothing could completely dampen my joy. I had just finished reading the three long letters from Jean that were waiting for me on my return from Guajara-Mirim. In the first was the stupendous news that she'd found a house. Thatched roof, bit of garden filled with flowers, rooms freshly whitewashed; secluded, not too fancy.

> *So, my darling, you can pedal those last 3,000 miles knowing that there's a place for you when you get back. The old Hibell, the lonely Hibell, is*

> *gone. You must know that.*
>
> *Sometimes I ask myself how it is you keep on. A tent for the tropics at 16,000 feet and you're still alive! What are you thinking and feeling? And yet I don't really need an answer because I can sense everything just as if I were still with you day and night . . .*

My leg had stiffened up almost to the point where I couldn't walk by the time they got me on to the operating table. The offending boil was cut out with no trouble, however, and all I had to endure was the paralysing pain of recovery. Two weeks I gave myself. Fortunately, I was befriended by a charming Brazilian couple I had met in hospital – a reporter and his wife – who couldn't seem to get enough of my stories. They took me home to recuperate, and in return for my board I obliged with a steady stream of chatter.

The day I rode out of Porto Velho it was raining. My leg was not fully healed, but I could bend it. Three days later I was pushing my bike up a hill, swatting at mosquitoes with my right hand. When I reached the top I rested and gazed out over the valley. Mist rose from the river. All around the jungle steamed. From the west, great black clouds were rolling in. A jagged sword flashed from the sky. Another. The dull percussion of thunder. An ominous shadow inked its way across the green. There came a spattering of rain followed by a blast of wind, and then the deluge. For the few brief moments it lasted, it was as if the sky and earth were joined in one horrendous cacophony. Rain slammed against slate. Lightning crackled, thunder boomed and roared. My ears rang. The universe seemed to cringe, wincing with pain.

At the top of the hill, I cautiously remounted my cycle, but it skidded from under me, and I almost fell. Sliding on the soles of my shoes, I came to a stop where some gravel had washed down from the bank. The earth was the colour of a cantaloupe, and as impossible to walk on as its flesh. I stood where I was and watched the transformation. Orange softened to pink and then dulled and became flecked with copper. I took a tentative step. The mud on my shoe was an inch thick. There was nothing to do but stand fast until the ground dried out. After a while the mud turned to a sort of potter's clay; and finally, in about an hour, I could ride again. By noon of the next day, the dust was back. There were 2500 kilometres of roads like this before I hit a paved one. When the rains came down in earnest, it would clearly be impossible to continue.

In ten days, however, I was beyond the Manaus junction. I had seen thunderstorms pass in the distance, had come upon sections of road where I had to wait for the mud to dry. But in the past week I had encountered only a single light shower. Then it poured. Vehicles were bogged down everywhere and I had to make an early camp. But the next day the road was dry enough for me to continue, and from then on conditions improved. Had I left the rains behind? It almost began to seem that I had. At each mail pick-up there were letters from Jean: warm, loving, wonderful letters which sustained me, but at the same time reminded me of my condition. How I longed for this journey to end.

One evening I was lying in my tent, staring at the floor in mindless misery, when much to my surprise I saw the floor move. I bent down for a closer look. It wasn't the floor, exactly, more like a leaf. And then I noticed that there were leaves all around – hundreds of them. All moving. And then one of the leaves started climbing up my leg and I felt a sharp stinging pain; and I realized that I was being invaded. Soldier ants! Swarming in everywhere. Those 'leaves' were pieces of my floor. I threw the food into a bag, grabbed my things, and dived out of the tent. Slapping the ants off with a towel, I managed to load everything on to the bike, and ride away. About 200 metres down the road was another clearing. I examined the ground carefully by candle-light. Satisfied that there were no ants, I spread out my poncho, got into my sleeping bag, and breathed a tentative sigh of relief. Where were the mosquitoes, I wondered? It was a beautiful night, stars gleaming brightly. I began to count my blessings. Soldier ants marched in columns that were sometimes four kilometres wide. They devoured everything: every leaf, every insect, every animal. What had I lost? Only my tent. And perhaps even that could be saved.

'Ow!' My head was on fire. Ants were crawling all over my shoulders. The road! Get to the road! Shivering, terrified, I squatted in the middle of the road. Ants don't like roads, I'd been told. Too hard for them to make their nests. I lay down on my sleeping bag. What if I fell asleep and a truck came by? Trucks don't travel at night. Not often, anyway. If one did, surely the driver would see me. Or I would hear him coming.

There was not an insect about. A gentle breeze cooled my brow. I curled up on my sleeping bag and let out a whopping great yawn. In less than a minute, I was asleep.

Chapter Thirteen

Three days later I found a woman with a sewing machine who was able to patch up my tent, but that very night the ants attacked again, destroying it beyond repair. Had this happened any earlier in the trip, I would have been desperate. But the miracle was that the mosquitoes seemed to have gone. It was as if I'd crossed an invisible boundary: mosquitoes here; soldier ants there. I could only hope that my 'luck' would continue.

As far as the rains were concerned, I was definitely in luck. I was chased, spattered, but only once deluged. By the time I reached Maraba on September 23rd, the atmosphere was pleasantly dry. The Brasilia–Belém road, all beautifully tarmaced, was now only 200 kilometres away. The countryside, which had been excruciatingly dull ever since leaving Peru, was much more interesting now; but I had thoughts only for home, and I cursed the mountain roads for slowing me down and hardly looked at the sights.

The first day on the paved road I did 120 kilometres. The following afternoon, I was riding along as near to the edge of the macadam as I dared, when a truck pulled alongside me. 'Here we go,' I thought, expecting glares and curses at the very least; perhaps beer in my face. As in Mexico, as in a thousand places all over the world, when one rides on a good highway, one always has to choose between the speed but danger of the macadam and the slowness but safety of the gravel shoulder. Particularly, it seemed, in Latin American countries, the sight of a cyclist brings out the worst in many drivers. Vehicles had swerved at me; even knocked me off the road.

The truck kept going, however, until its rear section was abreast of me. It was carrying gravel; there was an Indian standing there, grinning demonically. Suddenly I was blind – choking, swerving. When I cleared the grit out of my eyes, I could see the truck just ahead of me. The lout who had dumped the shovelful of gravel into my face was standing there as if daring me on. So up I came, faster than he'd planned by the look of his face. I don't know what I had in mind; to pass him, I suppose. At any rate I had my head bent over and my eyes as nearly shut as possible. I was up by the cab, now, going for all I was worth. Suddenly the truck put on a spurt, and this time he practically hit me in the face with his shovel. I careered to a stop. It took me several minutes before I could see again. But now I was out to kill.

The truck was about half a mile ahead, waiting for the on-coming traffic to get by so it could make a left turn. I pulled up in front of it, jumped off my bike, ran back to the passenger's side of the cab, and jerked open the door. The driver was huddled against the far side, looking scared. I grabbed him by the leg and pulled him down on to the road. I'd taken a couple of good punches at him and was about to slam him again when I felt a terrible blow on my back. It was my friend with the shovel. There was a demented look in his eyes now, as if he were confronting a mad dog. He raised the shovel over his head. I took a step backwards. And tripped. Now I was in for it: lying on my back, helpless. He was about to bash my brains out. With all my strength, I yelled out '*Bastante!*' Enough! The madness drained from his eyes, he pulled his mate into the truck, and they drove off.

I was weak from rage – and fear, and relief; but angry enough, also, so that once I staggered to my feet I approached the small crowd that had gathered and demanded their names. I needed witnesses, I said. But no one obliged. In a few minutes, in fact, they had all scattered. I had planned to ride to the nearest police station to make my complaint, but what was the point now? I could not even identify the truck properly. I stood there for a while, wondering what to do. And then the thought struck me: what a fool I'd been to take a chance like that. Would anyone have cared if I'd been killed? Would it even have been reported? They would have rolled me into a ditch or thrown me into a clump of trees – a meal for vultures and stray dogs. Jean would never have known what had happened to me. Nor would Mum and Dad. Feeling suddenly very weak, I got back on to my bicycle. Ride easy, Hibell, I told myself. On the gravel if you have to.

The pleasure of receiving mail is increased several fold if, instead of simply devouring it, instantly, at the post office, you transport it carefully to somewhere comfortable and relatively private – a pleasant café, for instance – and savour its sweetness over a cup of coffee or a glass of beer. In Belém, four days later, I chose a table near the window where I could keep an eye on my bike, drank down half of my first beer, and then opened Jean's letter. She had something important to communicate, she wrote. Was I sitting down? I took a good gulp, then read on. 'Well, here goes, darling. Jumping in at the deep end, I have to tell you that I'm well and truly pregnant; in fact, at the end of September, I'll be six months round.'

I sat there for a minute trying to take it in. Me? A father? I read the sentence again. I was a father! This was my baby! How had it happened? Was it really true? I read the rest of the letter, then re-read it. She wasn't pulling my leg. She was 'six months round'. She said so!

I looked around. Nothing had changed in the restaurant. There was my waiter, a tray held up over his head. I hopped up, excitedly. '*Moi, je suis père!*' The waiter held his tray up higher. '*Padre!* Me!' I pointed to myself. 'Papa! Father!'

The waiter nodded abstractly. 'Sí. La cuente. Momento.'

'No, no,' I said. 'Baby. Me. *Bebé. Un fils. Mi esposa bambino. Casa.*' I was so excited I couldn't remember a word of Portuguese.

'Ah, *bebé!*' He beamed at me. By this time he had served his customers, a family of six. I took him by the arm and tried to dance him around, but he politely detached himself and escaped to the kitchen.

I looked around for another ear, any ear. There were two people by my bicycle, examining it. I bounded out. 'I'm going to be a father!' I shouted.

'Jolly good,' the man replied. 'Heartily recommend it.'

'I've always wanted to be one, you see. But I've always travelled.'

The Swanleys were from Devon, it turned out. They were members of the International Bicycling Touring Society, in Belém on a business visit. I brought them back with me into the restaurant to celebrate. 'Beer?'

'Certainly not,' said Horace. 'We must have champagne.' The manager was called over, the situation explained. Yes, they had a bottle of Piper-Heidsieck, 1967. A good year.

Six months. She was already six months along. That meant by January I'd be a real father.

'Mr Hibell,' said Mrs Swanley, 'may I call you Ian? You must tell us, what will you do next? Something thrilling, no doubt.'

'China, Russia, West Africa?' mumbled Horace.

'Mr Hibell . . .'

It wasn't the Swanleys across the table from me now, but Jean. 'Cheerio, pet,' I said to her, and winked. She'd got plumper, of course. Waddled about like a penguin, no doubt.

'Antarctica,' I said. 'Perhaps we'll go there.'

'Oh, I say,' said Horace. 'That really would be something.'

'Or maybe I'll open a cycle shop.' They both looked appalled, as if the Queen had just told them what she really wanted to be was a pop singer.

Vladivostok to Omsk: the Trans-Siberian railway route. I'd always dreamed of doing that. Have to wait till later, I supposed. When Jamie was old enough to ride. Everything in Siberia on a monumental scale: mountains more rugged, plains vaster, lakes like inland seas. Roads? Gravel mostly, corduroyed in places. Jean would love that. But hold on – no need to wait that long. Easier, in fact, when he was still just a nipper. Or *she!*

'You'd soon grow tired of that,' said Mrs Swanley. 'Wouldn't he, Horace?'

'You're probably right,' I said. Imagine her keeping it secret from me all this time! How tempted she must have been to spill it all out. There was still the ride to Recife: ten days. Two more on the bus to Brasilia. Then home.

'If you must stay at home and be domestic, why not take

your fans out on tours? The Lake Country, say.'

'You could count on us, certainly.'

I saw her standing there at the barrier, reeling me in with her eyes. I was walking towards her, briskly. Then running. Then we were in each other's arms. We'd take the train back to Ashbury, get married right away. 'Ian will be over the moon,' she'd told her mother.

Well, of course I was.

A selection of bestsellers from SPHERE

FICTION

MONIMBO	Arnaud de Borchgrave and Robert Moss	£2.25 □
KING OF DIAMONDS	Carolyn Terry	£2.50 □
SPRING AT THE WINGED HORSE	Ted Willis	£1.95 □
TRINITY'S CHILD	William Prochnau	£2.50 □
THE SINISTER TWILIGHT	J. S. Forrester	£1.95 □

FILM & TV TIE-INS

SPROCKETT'S CHRISTMAS TALE	Louise Gikow	£1.75 □
THE DOOZER DISASTER	Michaela Muntean	£1.75 □
THE DUNE STORYBOOK	Joan D. Vinge	£2.50 □
ONCE UPON A TIME IN AMERICA	Lee Hays	£1.75 □
WEMBLEY FRAGGLE GETS THE STORY	Deborah Perlberg	£1.50 □

NON-FICTION

PRINCESS GRACE	Steven Englund	£2.50 □
BARRY FANTONI'S CHINESE HOROSCOPES		£1.95 □
THE COMPLETE HANDBOOK OF PREGNANCY	Wendy Rose-Neil	£5.95 □
WHO'S REALLY WHO	Compton Miller	£2.95 □
THE STOP SMOKING DIET	Jane Ogle	£1.50 □

All Sphere books are available at your local bookshop or newsagent, or can be ordered direct from the publisher. Just tick the titles you want and fill in the form below.

Name _____

Address _____

_____

Write to Sphere Books, Cash Sales Department, P.O. Box 11, Falmouth, Cornwall TR10 9EN

Please enclose a cheque or postal order to the value of the cover price plus:

UK: 55p for the first book, 22p for the second book and 14p for each additional book ordered to a maximum charge of £1.75.

OVERSEAS: £1.00 for the first book plus 25p per copy for each additional book.

BFPO & EIRE: 55p for the first book, 22p for the second book plus 14p per copy for the next 7 books, thereafter 8p per book.

Sphere Books reserve the right to show new retail prices on covers which may differ from those previously advertised in the text or elsewhere, and to increase postal rates in accordance with the PO.